The DOLPHINS of SHARK BAY

FOR TRAVIS —P.S.T.
TO CHRISTOPHER AND ANTARCTICA JAMES —S.T.

All images by Scott Tuason except for those on the following pages: I (OzStock Images), 4 (Ewa Krzyszczyk, Shark Bay Dolphin Project), 8 (Richard Woldendorp), 9 (Shutterstock), 10 (JTB Photo, Glow Images), 11 (top—Janet Mann, Shark Bay Dolphin Project; bottom—iStockphotoLP), 13 (Ewa Krzyszczyk, Shark Bay Dolphin Project), 14 (top—©Big Wave Productions Ltd.; bottom—Alison True), 16 (Vincent Leduc, Glow Images), 18 (top—Pamela S. Turner; bottom—Ewa Krzyszczyk, Shark Bay Dolphin Project), 22 (Ewa Krzyszczyk, Shark Bay Dolphin Project), 25 (Eric M. Patterson, Shark Bay Dolphin Project), 26 (Ewa Krzyszczyk, Shark Bay Dolphin Project), 27 (Pamela S. Turner), 28 (Yi-Jiun Jean Tsai, Shark Bay Dolphin Project), 29 (top—Eric M. Patterson, Shark Bay Dolphin Project), 30 (bottom left—©Big Wave Productions Ltd.; bottom right—Janet Mann, Shark Bay Dolphin Project), 31 (Ewa Krzyszczyk, Shark Bay Dolphin Project), 38 (Shark Bay Ecosystem Research Project), 39 (©Big Wave Productions Ltd.), 44 (bottom left—Jenny Smith, Shark Bay Dolphin Project; bottom right—Katie Gill, Shark Bay Dolphin Project), 49 (Carl Buell), 54 (Maggie Stanton, Shark Bay Dolphin Project), 57 (Ewa Krzyszczyk, Shark Bay Dolphin Project), 64 (Pamela S. Turner), 66 (Pamela S. Turner), 66 (Pamela S. Turner), 68 (Ewa Krzyszczyk, Shark Bay Dolphin Project), 70 (Simon Allen, Shark Bay Dolphin Project), 72 (Pamela S. Turner), 74 (Shutterstock).

The Library of Congress has cataloged the hardcover edition as follows:
Turner, Pamela S.
The dolphins of Shark Bay / by Pamela S. Turner.
p. cm.
Audience: Ages 10–14.
Audience: Grades 7–8.
1. Bottlenose dolphin—Behavior—Australia—Shark Bay (W.A.)—Juvenile literature.
2. Bottlenose dolphin—Research—Australia—Shark Bay (W.A.)—Juvenile literature. 3. Mann, Janet—Juvenile literature. I. Title.
QL737.C432T87 2013
599.53'3—dc23
2012048463

ISBN: 978-0-547-71638-1 hardcover
ISBN: 978-0-544-80909-3 paperback

Manufactured in China
SCP 10 9 8 7 6 5 4 3 2 1
4500595909

The DOLPHINS of SHARK BAY

by **Pamela S. Turner**

With photographs by Scott Tuason

Houghton Mifflin Harcourt
Boston New York

Standing on the *Pomboo*'s dashboard gives Janet a better view of the surrounding waters.

CHAPTER ONE

MYSTERY DOLPHIN

Janet Mann stands on the dashboard of the *Pomboo*, bare toes gripping the steering wheel. She spots a gray fin in the distance.

"Unknown dolphin," the biologist calls. After twenty-five years in Shark Bay, Western Australia, Janet recognizes hundreds of wild bottlenose dolphins by the unique nicks and cuts on their dorsal fins. This animal, however, is a stranger.

Janet angles the *Pomboo*'s bow toward the dolphin. Not quite directly, though. She never wants a dolphin to feel chased or threatened.

"Does it have a sponge?" Janet asks. "Can anybody see?"

Mystery Dolphin dives before we can get a good look. Janet scrambles off her perch and cuts the engine. Sound carries far across flat water; without the thrum of the motor we might hear the dolphin's breath as it resurfaces. We are silent and tense, every ear straining for that distinctive *poooff*. With our faces pressed into binoculars we look like a boatload of windblown raccoons.

Poooff. Mystery Dolphin rises; a brown blob covers its nose like an oven mitt. Happy dances break out at this odd sight.

"A new sponger—"

"Awesome—"

Mystery Dolphin carries a basket sponge on its rostrum.

"This is *so* cool!"

Janet, graduate student Eric Patterson, and project assistant Jenny Smith are all talking at once and slapping high-fives. Mystery Dolphin goes back to its business in the channel below.

Just as we humans are using tools (for us, a boat and binoculars), this dolphin is too. Some Shark Bay dolphins use a squishy sea sponge to protect their nose (called the rostrum) as they rummage along a channel bottom. When a sponging dolphin flushes a fish hiding in the rubble, the dolphin drops the sponge and snatches its prey.

Sponging dolphins possess a scarce talent. Tool use—that most human of talents—is extremely rare among wild animals. Some chimpanzees use sticks to collect termites, some crows use twigs to stab beetle larvae, and some sea otters use rocks to smash shellfish. Dolphins have no fingers, no feet, no paws. Yet somehow, in a brilliant stroke of cetacean innovation, Shark Bay dolphins have discovered how to use a sponge as a tool.

Scientists classify bottlenose dolphins as cetaceans (see-TAY-shuns), members of the scientific order Cetacea (see-TAY-sha). Cetacea includes seventy-seven species of whales and dolphins.

Monkey Mia

Peron Point

Shark Bay

AUSTRALIA

Brisbane

Perth

Sydney

Melbourne

The two fingers of Shark Bay cover 3,900 square miles (10,000 square kilometers). On the land surrounding the bay, plants and animals from Australia's hot, dry north mix with those of the cooler, damper south. The bay's waters are a meeting place for marine plants and animals from the warm Indian Ocean and the chilly Southern Ocean. An estimated 3,000 to 4,000 bottlenose dolphins live in Shark Bay.

Shark Bay bottlenose dolphins are the only known tool-using dolphins anywhere in the world. Janet has documented sponging by fifty-four Shark Bay dolphins; our newly discovered animal is number fifty-five.

Maybe it's no great surprise that dolphins have invented the nose mitt. After all, everyone knows that these animals are smart. For years, captive bottlenoses have entranced aquarium visitors with perfectly timed backflips, corkscrew jumps, and tail walks. Decades of research on captive dolphins reveals much more: Dolphins can learn simple artificial languages and can recognize themselves in a mirror (a key test of self-awareness). They quickly grasp the meaning of pointing (chimpanzees don't) and are excellent vocal mimics (chimpanzees aren't).

Dolphins also understand abstract ideas. One researcher taught two captive bottlenose dolphins a "tandem" command and used it with other commands to ask the dolphins to do things together. Then he taught the dolphins a "create" command: *Show me something I haven't seen before*. The very first time the researcher gave his dolphins the "tandem" and "create" commands together, the dolphins dove to the bottom of the pool—apparently for a planning session. A moment later the duo leaped out of the water in perfect sync, both spurting water from their mouths.

Dolphins are even smart enough to train their trainers. One scientist rewarded her study dolphin with a fish when the dolphin responded to

Other animal species also use tools. However, the sponging dolphins of Shark Bay devote more time to tool use than any other animal besides humans.

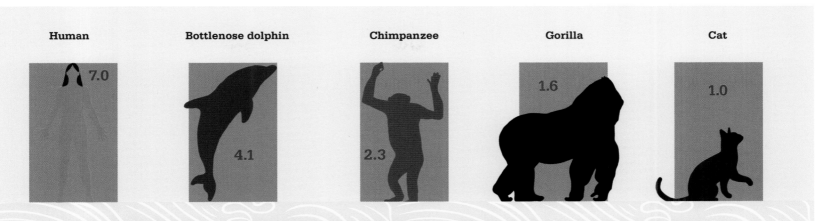

Human	Bottlenose dolphin	Chimpanzee	Gorilla	Cat
7.0	4.1	2.3	1.6	1.0

Scientists use a measure called the encephalization quotient (en-SEF-a-la-ZAY-shun QWO-shunt), or EQ, to compare the relative braininess of different species. EQ compares brain size to body size for many different mammals. If a mammal has an average brain-to-body weight, its EQ is 1.

commands. If it refused to respond, the scientist turned her back and walked away. One day the scientist accidentally rewarded the dolphin with a spiny-tailed type of fish that the dolphin hated. The dolphin spat it out, swam to the other side of the pool, and hung vertically in the water with her back to the scientist. Time-outs can cut both ways.

Dolphins have such a brainy reputation that some people dream that if we could just create the right computer program to decode their clicks and whistles, we could talk to them. Maybe we could discuss important questions. *What is the meaning of life? Do we have free will, or only the illusion of free will? Is the hokey pokey REALLY what it's all about?*

Yes, dolphins are smart. But *why* are they smart? How did such a sophisticated mind arise in the ocean? A bottlenose dolphin's brain is three times the size of a chimpanzee's. What is all that brainpower *for*?

The answers to these questions can't be found in a concrete tank. If you want to know why dolphins are smart, you must ask: What is happening out in the wild, in the dolphins' natural environment? Why does a dolphin *need* to be smart?

For more than twenty-five years Janet Mann and her colleagues have recorded the lives of hundreds of wild dolphins for the Shark Bay Dolphin Project. Among these dolphins are good mothers and bad, friends and rivals, innovators and failures, charmers and schemers. Using sponges as tools is just one of the astonishingly odd, creative, and intelligent things these wild animals do.

Why are dolphins smart?

The dolphins you are about to meet may have the answers.

Five-year-old Shiver (top) and two-year-old Samu glide through the waters off the Monkey Mia beach. Mia (MY-ah) is an Australian aboriginal word for "shelter." No one knows for sure why it's called "Monkey" Mia.

CHAPTER TWO

MONKEY MIA

Most of what we know about dolphins comes from captive animals, for a very good reason—wild dolphins are difficult to study. They surface, breathe, and vanish. The next sighting might be hundreds of yards away. Although most dolphin behavior happens underwater, snorkeling or scuba diving doesn't help much. If a human invades the water near a wild dolphin, the animal will either bolt or (less likely) stop and stare. Neither is helpful if you want to see normal dolphin behavior.

In the early 1980s two young Americans scientists, Richard Connor and Rachel Smolker, heard about a spot in Western Australia that offered a unique opportunity to study dolphins in the wild. The directions were simple: Fly to Perth, the most isolated city of its size in the world. Keep the Indian Ocean on your left as you drive north. After a dusty day of dodging kangaroos, arrive at a scruffy fishing camp with a weird name: Monkey Mia. You'll find lots of wild dolphins . . . and a few of them will even take a fish right out of your hand.

Richard and Rachel had been studying the dolphins around Monkey Mia on and off for several years when Janet arrived in 1988. "The road linking Monkey Mia to the nearest town was dirt in those days, full of potholes," Janet recalls. "It was night when I got there, and totally dark. Monkey Mia was just a campground with a bunch of tents and lots of snoring."

to Peron Point

Red Cliff Bay

Monkey Mia

The next morning, Janet opened her tent flap. She had a view of pale sand, blue water, and gray fins.

Wild dolphins had visited Monkey Mia for decades, thanks to fishermen who tossed a fish or two to a passing bottlenose. By 1988 a dozen animals regularly visited the beach to accept handouts. It was a dolphin lover's paradise. "I waded out into the water and a young dolphin came up and started petting me with her pectoral fin," Janet recalls. "Some of the dolphins loved to play keep-away with bits of sea grass, too. You could swim out with a piece and a dolphin would grab it. Then you had to try to get it back."

Puck and Nicky, two young females, spent most of their time around Monkey Mia. "Puck was amazingly gentle, always the nice one," Janet says. "Often Puck would politely accept a fish from a tourist and appear to swallow it. Then she swam a few meters away and coughed the fish back up. She seemed to be genuinely interested in people. If you dropped a hat in the water, she'd want to play catch with it."

An aerial photo of Monkey Mia and Red Cliff Bay reveals the diversity of marine habitats within Shark Bay. Pale areas are shallow sand flats; deeper water is dark blue; and the dark, ruffled patches are sea-grass beds.

Nicky, on the other hand, was the nippy one. "Nicky and some of the males would bite people," Janet says. "Nicky just seemed to be in it for the fish."

Richard and Rachel had been identifying and observing the dolphins by taking photos of their fins and following the dolphins in a small dinghy. Richard was studying the adult males while Rachel was working on dolphin communication. Janet planned to focus on females and calves.

Shark Bay offered the researchers ideal conditions. The local dolphins were accustomed to small boats, and the calm, shallow water (average depth: sixteen to twenty feet, or five to six meters) made dolphin watching relatively easy. In this remote spot Janet and her colleagues could observe the second-brainiest creature on planet Earth. Figuring out how to make sense of their observations, however, was another matter. That required the help of African baboons.

Nicky in the shallows off Monkey Mia. Dolphins have very good vision, both underwater and in air. Their in-air vision works best at long distances (probably to spot faraway sea birds diving into schools of fish), but their underwater vision works best close up (to target individual prey).

As a child, Janet didn't imagine a future full of blue horizons. Instead she dreamed of dark shapes moving through the green-filtered light of African forests.

"I wanted to be Jane Goodall," she says. "I wanted to be a primatologist, someone who studies apes and monkeys. Everyone made fun of me. They said, 'It's just a phase. You'll grow out of it.'"

But she didn't. Janet wrote to Dr. Goodall and to Jeanne Altmann, a primatologist famous for her studies of savanna baboons. Professor Altmann wrote back, and Janet never forgot that small kindness.

In high school Janet considered becoming an archaeologist (a scientist who studies the remains of past human societies). After all, she reasoned, people are primates too.

Janet landed a summer job measuring deer bones from a prehistoric garbage dump. Unfortunately, she found the work incredibly boring. One afternoon, as she dozed atop her skeleton pile, the archaeologist walked in. Janet jerked awake and tried to look busy.

"Were you sleeping?" her boss asked.

"No," Janet lied.

Bottlenose dolphins like Puck (head raised) are divided into two species: the common bottlenose (*Tursiops truncatus*) and the Indo-Pacific bottlenose (*Tursiops aduncus*). DNA studies suggest that Shark Bay dolphins have a mixed genetic heritage—part common, part Indo-Pacific.

"Hmmm." The archaeologist peered at the deer bone–shaped dents on Janet's cheeks and forehead. "Janet, maybe archaeology isn't for you."

Back to apes and monkeys.

As a college student at Brown University, Janet applied to work on a baboon study led by her childhood idol, Jeanne Altmann. Professor Altmann had never allowed anyone as young as Janet to work in Africa, but she recognized Janet's passion and dedication.

Janet lived for a year in a Kenyan game park filled with lions, leopards, and elephants. She collected data on savanna baboons for Professor Altmann's long-term mother-infant study.

Professor Altmann was already famous for changing the way scientists look at animals in the wild. A scientist trying to record animal behavior must make decisions, especially when observing animals mingling in a social group. Which ones should be observed? Which actions should be recorded? Before Professor Altmann, most researchers recorded whatever was most noticeable. Snarling males attract attention. Quietly grooming females don't.

Big mistake.

Imagine that you're trying to take a sample of jellybeans from a big jar with equal numbers of colored candies. If you grab the eye-catching red while ignoring everything else, you won't end up with a fair representation of what's in the jar. In science terms, your cherry jellybeans would be a "biased sample."

Professor Altmann taught Janet to collect in-depth data on everything that flavored a baboon's life. All that calm picking-through-each-other's-fur business was part of a female social network. And social rank (revealed by who groomed whom) mattered. Higher-status female baboons were the most successful moms. They raised the most babies.

Baboons use grooming to express social bonds.

Relentless work in a remote place isn't for everyone, but it can be the lens that focuses the future. "Kenya changed my life," Janet says simply.

She returned home with wild hair and elephant dung still caked on her shoes. "My family was a little afraid of me," Janet confesses. Weeks passed before she could attend a college party without seeing her classmates as hyperactive, hyperweird baboons. Yet she knew she'd found her calling.

She began graduate studies in animal behavior at the University of Michigan. To receive a Ph.D., a graduate student needs a big research project. By coincidence, the University of Michigan had just become involved with a dolphin study in Australia. So Janet, the girl who loved primates, took the long flight west and followed the long road north to a place called Monkey Mia that didn't have any monkeys.

But it did have dolphins.

On Monkey Mia's craziest days, several hundred visitors crowded the shallows to feed, pet, and photograph the dolphins. The beach resembled a movie premiere with no velvet ropes to keep the fans from the stars. In the chaos, things sometimes got rough. Three male dolphins, in particular, were notorious for knocking people down and snapping at arms and legs.

However, the dolphins suffered worse from such close human-dolphin contact. Just months after Janet's arrival, a leaky sewage tank fouled the beach. Seven dolphins disappeared and were presumed dead of bacterial infections. A new sewage system was installed, but the free-for-all feedings continued. Dolphin tourism provided jobs for local people. Many of them feared that any limits on dolphin feeding would destroy their livelihoods. Others pointed out that destroying dolphins wasn't great for dolphin tourism, either.

Amid the controversy, Janet dove into her long-term study of dolphin mothers and calves. Wild dolphins live in what scientists call a "fission-fusion" society. That means dolphins gather in small groups, but group membership changes constantly as animals come and go. Females, calves, and juveniles typically gather together while adult males form their own groups. Janet studied as many mom-calf pairs as she could find. Some of the dolphins she observed visited the beach to beg for fish. Many didn't.

Janet's African methods transferred surprisingly well. Like mother baboons, mother dolphins must feed themselves and support their offspring. They must avoid predators and navigate social relationships. Janet followed mother-calf pairs around in a small boat and gathered data using the same basic sampling methods she'd learned from Professor Altmann.

By sampling the behavior of dozens of mothers and calves, Janet could study maternal (motherly) care in dolphins and learn how calves grow and develop skills. She also spent part of every year studying human mothers and infants in the United States. After being awarded a Ph.D., Janet continued her research as a university professor in the United States and returned to Shark Bay every year to gather more data.

Each spring (September to November in Australia) Janet looked forward to calf-birthing season. One day in 1992, Puck was swimming around with a Santa Claus belly. The next day she was a slim mother with a little squirt by her side.

At first Puck's newborn daughter, Piccolo, bobbed to the surface like a cork. A baby dolphin needs a week or so to master the graceful

A Shark Bay newborn swims next to its mother. Baby dolphins, called calves, are usually born tail first so the baby doesn't have to hold its breath too long during the birthing. When it first emerges, a newborn's dorsal fin is as floppy as a puppy's ear, which eases the baby's way through the birth canal.

roll-up-and-breathe that adult dolphins perform so effortlessly. Puck stayed close—partly to be on hand to help Piccolo if needed, partly to stay between her calf and any dangers lurking below, and partly to foil calf-nappers.

During the first week or so, a newborn instinctively follows anything moving in front of it. Usually that's Mom. However, sometimes a young female dolphin can't resist the urge to take a neighbor's new baby out for a spin. If another dolphin lures her infant away, the baby's mother gives chase, jerking her head and clapping her jaw at the offender (translation: *Knock it off!*) before retrieving her clueless child.

After a week or two, Piccolo's mom-recognition and swimming skills improved. This was a big relief for Puck, who was probably exhausted.

Janet's mother-calf study revealed that 44 percent of calves don't live past weaning (usually age three or four). Life in Shark Bay isn't easy. Yet the overall dolphin population is stable, so the calf mortality (death) rate of 44 percent is normal for life in the wild. Other long-lived species such as chimpanzees and gorillas have similar infant mortality rates.

The really disturbing data, however, came from the beach-begging females. From 1986 to 1994, eleven of fifteen calves died. That's a death rate of 73 percent—far higher than normal. Puck's daughter Piccolo was one of the few survivors.

One calf's death haunted everyone at Monkey Mia. As her mother begged along the beach, a four-month-old infant was waiting about 230 feet (70 meters) offshore. A large tiger shark attacked, biting the baby's tail flukes and belly. The calf's panicked whistles sent its mom and several other dolphins charging to its defense. Though they chased the shark away, it was too late.

The mother pushed and prodded the calf's lifeless body. She whistled constantly, as if begging her baby, *Wake up! Breathe!*

After a heartbreaking hour, Janet and her colleagues removed the corpse from the water. An exam revealed that the calf was already half starved and sick with a lung infection. It probably would have died anyway.

Tourists gave the beach-fed mothers so much food, they looked bloated. Why didn't their calves thrive?

Janet's data held the answer. She looked at how the beach-fed mothers and their calves behaved near the beach versus away from the beach.

Puck with her newest calf, Samu, one day after the calf's birth. Dolphins and humans are both mammals. They breathe air; their babies are born alive and drink milk; and they have hair. Baby dolphins are born with a few hair follicles on their rostrum that soon fall off.

A newborn Shark Bay calf pops up to breathe beside its mom. A bottlenose dolphin pregnancy lasts twelve months; females give birth to single calves spaced about four years apart. Adult male dolphins don't help with calf rearing.

Away from the beach, they acted like normal mother-calf pairs—except that beach-fed mothers sometimes approached fishing boats to beg. At the Monkey Mia beach, however, their behavior changed. Instead of hunting, nursing their calves, or protecting them from sharks, the mothers spent hours obsessively begging. Fat moms didn't necessarily raise well-fed calves, and the calves of beach-fed mothers didn't learn the foraging skills they needed in order to survive. Tourists assumed that their fish handouts were helpful. Instead, Monkey Mia's baby dolphins starved in a stew of good intentions.

Becoming overly relaxed around people created other hazards too. One day Janet watched Nicky and Puck as they fed on mullet (a kind of schooling fish) that were trying to escape from a fisherman's net. Nicky and her calf left; Janet followed. She looked back toward Puck but saw only two-year-old Piccolo racing back and forth.

Where's Puck? Janet scanned the water. A bulge in the net pushed up and down. It was Puck's dorsal fin. She was trapped by the heavy net, unable to raise her blowhole high enough to breathe. Janet raced her boat back. Little Piccolo's frantic whistles could be heard even above water.

"Cut your net—you've got a dolphin!" she screamed at the fisherman. "Puck's drowning! *Get her out!*"

Janet searched for a knife. "I was frantic," she recalls. "Ready to dive in."

Instead of slashing his net, the fisherman grabbed the edge and heaved, lifting Puck halfway out of the water. The strands tightened and cut.

"Puck is the mellowest of dolphins," Janet says, remembering that awful moment. "But the look in her eye—sheer terror."

The fisherman pulled again; Puck unspooled and raced away. Bright blood ribboned the water behind her. Piccolo bolted too. Janet trailed them until Puck slowed and Janet saw, to her great relief, that Puck's wounds had finally stopped bleeding.

Puck's lack of wariness almost killed her. And if she had drowned, little Piccolo would have died too. Something needed to be done to save Puck, Piccolo, and the other Monkey Mia beach dolphins.

On a softly clouded morning seventeen years later, I'm waiting on a pier in the prime position for dolphin watching at Monkey Mia. That is, standing next to Janet.

Fins carousel through the water a few yards away. Janet names each dorsal: There's Piccolo, Puck's daughter. She's all grown up now, with two daughters of her own, Flute and Eden. Piccolo's belly bulges slightly with a new baby, due in a few months. There's Kiya, Puck's other grown daughter, and Puck's adolescent son, India.

Puck swims in the middle of her large family. Janet points out Puck's two-year-old son, Samu, tucked against his mother's side. This calf may be thirty-six-year-old Puck's last infant.

The dolphin in the foreground was attacked by a shark when he was a calf. His peduncle (the area behind his dorsal fin) was deeply scarred by the shark's bite.

"Puck's a terrific mom," Janet tells me. "All of her kids adore her. They stay very close and never want to leave."

The affection in Janet's voice is obvious. I instantly adore Puck too. That's the thing about dolphins: they are so easy to love.

The red dirt road to Monkey Mia is now paved; a resort and restaurant line the shore. Barefoot moms and dads, kids and grandparents, are gathered at the water's edge to await the dolphins. Puck's clan draws near. The crowd gasps: a collective voice of wordless awe.

Puck glides close to the water's edge. Piccolo joins her mother, and the two swim lazy curves around a Shark Bay park ranger standing in two-feet-deep water. Grandfathers lift toddlers atop their shoulders, and teenage girls clutch hands. Wild dolphins! Three steps away!

The crowd listens as the ranger explains how unregulated feedings ended in 1995. With Janet's help, the Australian government put new

Puck at the Monkey Mia beach. Scars from her fishnet accident mark her head and neck.

rules in place. Males are no longer fed, because they are too aggressive. Young dolphins never get fish either; this forces them to learn hunting skills. The rangers now offer three half-hour feedings each morning, and only five adult females are fed. Each receives only a few fish. This encourages the mothers to spend most of their day doing normal dolphin things. Their offspring are learning survival skills, and mortality is now very low.

The danger of net entanglement has lessened too. After Puck's trauma, local fishermen agreed to cast their nets farther offshore.

Puck and Piccolo skim along the edge of the crowd. What must they think of puckered pink toes and clicking cameras?

The younger members of Puck's clan mingle in deeper water off the pier. "India's such a mama's boy," Janet says. "It's time he went off and joined other males. But he'd rather hang out with the family."

Seven-year-old India still shows plenty of male bravado. He mock-charges eight-year-old Eden, veering off at the last moment. She takes evasive action; he repeats the maneuver. Five-year-old Flute zips over to Eden. Flute's pectoral fin rests reassuringly on her big sister's side as they swim in tandem.

Janet smiles. "Piccolo's girls stick together."

Samu flips over on his back and swims belly-up just under the water. Slivers of silver catch the sun—tiny baitfish trapped against the surface. Samu picks them off, one by one, with little snaps of his jaws.

This technique is called snacking. A calf's cone-shaped teeth sprout within a few weeks after birth. Within a few months a calf begins "play snacking," chasing and capturing blades of sea grass before progressing to actual moving fish. Snacking on tiny baitfish is like eating sunflower seeds one by one; it won't fill Samu's belly. But snacking helps Samu master basic hunting skills. He'll nurse for at least another year (probably several) as he learns more advanced skills from Puck.

Puck doesn't share the fish she catches with Samu. Most Shark Bay prey are small, caught one at a time and swallowed quickly to prevent the prey from escaping. But dolphins are great imitators. Calves such as Samu probably learn most hunting techniques through a mix of trial and error and imitation. Janet says that when Samu was smaller, Puck did a lot of snacking. Dolphin see, dolphin do.

New dorsal fins appear off the beach. "That's Surprise and her adult daughter, Shock," says Janet. "And Nicky with her calf, Fin."

Instead of pausing to greet the other dolphins, Nicky arrows into the shallows. Three-year-old Fin wanders off toward Samu. Fin is undersized—no bigger than Samu, though she's more than a year older. The two play tag around the pier.

Down on the beach, park volunteers arrive with five fish buckets. Each bears the name of a beach-fed female: PUCK, PICCOLO, NICKY, SURPRISE, and SHOCK. The dolphins know the drill. Each moves calmly into position as the volunteers select a few people from the crowd. These lucky ones feed a fish to a dolphin. Smiles spread and cameras are raised.

Puck, Piccolo, Surprise, and Shock are attentive, hard-working moms. Since 1995 Puck has lost one infant—probably to a shark. Every other calf born to these four females has survived.

And then there's Nicky.

Janet sighs. "Nicky's a lousy mom. She ignores her calves. When they try to get into nursing position, she'll often turn away. Not a single one of Nicky's calves has made it to adulthood."

Janet is the sort of person who will cross the street to pet an arthritic, half-blind golden retriever. She can't even resist petting drug-sniffing dogs at airports. ("I got yelled at for that," she confesses.) But she clearly can't dredge up warm fuzzies for Nicky.

Janet explains that Nicky has a sister who is a successful mom with two adult offspring and a grandchild. Yet the two don't socialize, which is very rare for sisters.

"Nicky doesn't care," Janet says. "She never joins with anybody. I feel so sorry for Fin, Nicky's calf. At least Puck's kids play with her."

Fin and Samu tire of chase games. The two twirl idly in the water making whoopee-cushion sounds, like bored children waiting for their mothers to finish shopping.

The volunteers holding fish buckets raise their hands one by one. This means that the bucket has only one fish remaining. Each dolphin will get its last fish at exactly the same time. This procedure keeps the dolphins from rushing to another bucket once theirs is empty. When the last fish are dispensed, the volunteers scoop water into their buckets and dump it out again. This little ceremony says, *No more fish*. Puck, Piccolo, Surprise,

Samu rubs Puck's head. Puck is thirty-six years old, elderly by dolphin standards. Shark Bay dolphins can live into their forties.

Young calves love to play with bits of sea grass, chasing and capturing them over and over. This play helps them master the art of "snacking."

Surprise nuzzles park ranger Alex Dent. People are no longer allowed to touch the dolphins at Monkey Mia, but sometimes the dolphins choose to touch people.

Nicky (top) and her daughter Fin. Calves like Fin usually wean at age three or four. By then their mother is often pregnant with another calf.

and Shock move into deeper water to linger and mingle.

Nicky angles off on her own path. She's self-centered, her kid needs foster care, and her own family won't have anything to do with her. Nicky may be a flawed mom, but she's the only one Fin has. The little calf follows.

Samu drops to Puck's side to nurse. After a few gulps Samu surfaces and grazes Puck with his pectoral fin, as if to say, *Thanks, Mom.*

With her extended family gathered around her, Puck heads off to hunt the mint-green waters off Monkey Mia. "Puck's a shallow-water special-ist. When she was nine years old, she was even seen carrying a sponge," Janet says. "Puck will try anything."

For a wild dolphin like Puck, success means passing your genes to the next generation. Yet fish can be difficult to catch. How does a hard-working single mom keep her baby alive?

"Females have to be creative," Janet explains. "They need fifty percent more food when they have a nursing calf to support."

Janet thinks maternal care played a role in the evolution of dolphin intelligence. If you have a problem to solve—*How can I find more food?*—a big brain can be a big asset. Yet sometimes clever females do more than just keep their calves alive. Sometimes they take dolphinkind in entirely new directions.

Dodger carries a basket sponge on her rostrum

CHAPTER THREE

MOTHERS OF INVENTION

I
t's as if Janet called ahead and made an appointment: *Sponging Demonstration, 10:00 a.m.* Eleven-year-old Dodger swims straight for the *Pomboo,* a bowl-shaped sponge cupped over her rostrum.

"Dodger's boat-friendly," Janet explains. "And she was the first third-generation sponger we ever saw. That was a huge thrill."

Our sweetheart sponger works the channel with professional ease: two breaths at the surface, a tail-up dive, down for a minute or so.

More than twenty-five years earlier a fisherman told Rachel Smolker, one of the first dolphin researchers at Shark Bay, about a dolphin that had a horrible growth on its face. Rachel worried about this poor disfigured creature. But when she found the dolphin, she realized the "growth" was actually a sponge. That first known sponger was Dodger's grandmother.

Rachel spotted several other sponge-carrying dolphins, mostly females with calves. All frequented the deeper channels that gouged Shark Bay's sandy flats and sea-grass beds. It wasn't obvious why the dolphins carried sponges, since they didn't seem to be eating them. A dolphin carried the same sponge around for an hour or so before discarding it.

Maybe the dolphins just liked to give the ocean floor a good scrub now and then. Maybe there were also squeegee-carrying dolphins!

Dodger with her sponge. Spongers don't begin sponging until age two or older because sponging requires long dives (two or three minutes) to hunt successfully. This diving pattern is too physically demanding for very young dolphins.

And dolphins looking for a place to plug in a vacuum cleaner!

Okay. Maybe not.

Researchers later spotted one of the sponge-carrying dolphins in clear shallow water. The dolphin poked and prodded the bottom . . . and away skipped a small fish. The dolphin dropped the sponge and gulped its prey.

Wild dolphins using *tools?* When this discovery was reported, scientists around the world spilled their morning coffee.

In the best tradition of science, however, this discovery raised more questions than it answered. Why do dolphins sponge instead of foraging in a more "normal" way? Why don't spongers use echolocation (dolphin sonar) to find prey? Why do some Shark Bay dolphins sponge and others don't?

Janet hoped to answer some of these questions. Her long-term mother-calf study included sponging females such as Dodger's mother and grandmother. But nobody had ever tracked the development of a sponger from birth to adulthood. To Janet's delight, Dodger's mother began carrying sponges at age two; Dodger also sponged at about the same age. Over the years Janet has watched many other offspring of spongers. She discovered that sponging is a family business. A dolphin masters sponging *only* if Mom also sponges. (A few dolphins such as Puck sometimes carry sponges, but they have been seen doing it only once—never twice—and they don't seem to know what to do with the sponge.)

Janet, Eric Patterson, and I watch Dodger sponge. This time she surfaces sixty-six feet (twenty meters) away. Dodger has a distinctively nicked and slightly tipsy dorsal fin, making the ID easy for a novice like me. Her head jerks slightly.

Eric frames Dodger in his binoculars. "She's gulping a fish. No sponge."

Dodger vanishes and reappears with her sponge. Down she goes again.

We're drifting over a murky thirty-three-foot-deep (ten-meter-deep) channel washed by a fast-flowing current. Not many people have seen

Dodger's workplace, but Eric is one of the few. Observing spongers from the surface can tell a scientist only so much. If you want to understand sponging, you've got to try it yourself. You've got to jump in and let the gray-green water close over your head.

"I kept all sorts of pets as a kid," Eric tells me. "Frogs, bugs in jars, birds, hamsters, dogs, cats. As many as my mom would allow."

Eric grew up in Colorado and went to college there too. He studied aerospace engineering because he liked math and science, and because people told him he would be able to get a job.

One day Eric listened to a talk given by a professor who studied animal play. Something that had dimmed switched on again. "I decided I wanted to study animals," Eric says. "Especially animals with smarts."

He enrolled in a Ph.D. program at Georgetown University. To receive his Ph.D., Eric must plan and carry out a major research project under Janet's supervision. His project is solving the mystery of what spongers are doing, and why.

Eric dives to the bottom of a sponger's channel using a hookah (the yellow hose connects to an air source floating at the surface). He cuts a sample from the basket sponge for later analysis.

Swift currents carry tiny bits of food to filter-feeding sponges clinging to the sides of Shark Bay's channels. Sand, broken coral, and rock cover the channel bottoms. Although Janet and Eric would love to film dolphins sponging in these channels, the murkiness and the difficulty of securing cameras in fast-flowing water make it difficult.

So instead, Eric has become a sponger. He sticks a sponge on a pole and rummages around the channel bottoms. Data from hundreds of Eric's dives have helped Janet and Eric understand what Dodger does. And why she *doesn't* use echolocation, her dolphin superpower.

Dolphin echolocation is one of the wonders of the biological world. As Dodger swims, she sends out pulses of clicks. When these clicks hit an object, the clicks echo back toward Dodger. Her brain processes the returning sounds. If she emits slower clicks she is using a "wide beam" search

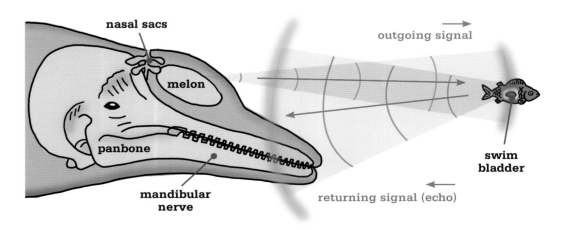

nasal sacs

outgoing signal

melon

panbone

mandibular nerve

returning signal (echo)

swim bladder

Dolphins emit pulses of clicks using their nasal sacs. Tissue in the dolphin's "melon" (inside its bulging forehead) acts as a lens that focuses the pulses. The clicks "tap" the target and bounce back. The dolphin absorbs the returning sounds through nerves in oil-filled spaces in its jaw. Those nerves send the information to the dolphin's inner ear and then on to the brain.

(*Is there a shark shape around?*). Faster clicks produce a focused "laser beam" that delivers astonishing detail (*A baitfish with a ragged fin!*).

Imagine being blindfolded. Three cups sit in front of you: one made of wood, one made of glass, and one made of brass. Someone taps each cup with a spoon. You can probably guess which is which by listening to the sounds generated by the tapping. You can also roughly guess the distance between you and the cups. And if someone tapped an empty cup and then a cup filled with water, you could probably tell the difference.

Dolphins like Dodger use their clicks to "tap" objects. Scientists think that the dolphin's brain converts the returning sounds into an "echo image"—an instant three-dimensional picture. Submerge those three imaginary cups in water, and instead of detecting simply "wood, glass, brass" and "full of air" or "full of liquid," a dolphin could *hear* the exact shape and thickness of each cup, *hear* exactly how full or empty each cup is, and *hear* the cups' exact location, too. Even in utter darkness.

Echolocation clicks also penetrate flesh. Scientists suspect that dolphins sometimes use echolocation to examine potential prey: *Is it edible?* When a young Shark Bay dolphin sees an adult carrying a fish in its mouth, the youngster will sometimes "buzz" the older dolphin's catch with bursts of clicks.

Scientists also think that dolphins may be able to see inside other dolphins' bodies. Dodger may know if another dolphin's stomach is empty, or if a female is carrying an unborn calf. A male may be able to tell if Dodger is in estrus (ready for mating). Dolphins may be transparent to one another in ways we can hardly imagine.

To learn about dolphin sponging, Eric patiently dove and poked and prodded the channel bottoms with his sponge pole. Jenny Smith, a project assistant and a recent graduate of the University of California, Santa Cruz, and Georgetown student Kipp Searles dove with him and videotaped his efforts. They used the film to identify everything Eric's sponging scared out of hiding.

By using echolocation, a dolphin such as Puck can locate prey in silty, murky water.

Pole sponging helps Eric and Janet understand why dolphins sponge.

(By the way, neither Dodger nor any other sponging dolphins ever stopped by to critique Eric's sponging. Janet and Eric assured me that Shark Bay dolphins never approach divers. But after they said this, guess who showed up during Eric's very next research dive, apparently hoping for an underwater handout? Nicky! She has great timing.)

Eric's sponging mostly flushed out one particular kind of fish: barred sand perch. Unlike most fish, sand perch don't have swim bladders. Swim bladders are pockets of gas that fish use to control their buoyancy. Because gases are less dense than the fish's flesh or the surrounding seawater, a swim bladder gives a nice echo when tapped with an echolocation click.

Dolphin echolocation is so fine-tuned that dolphins can probably identify different kinds of fish by the different echoes given off by their swim bladders. Fish that lack swim bladders, like the barred sand perch, are harder to detect.

Eric found many barred sand perch hiding in the jumble of rock and shell that litters the channel bottoms. Dolphin sonar can penetrate a few inches into smooth sand, but rocky rubble is a problem. There's too much "noise" in the returning echo.

A barred sand perch in Shark Bay.

So the bottom of sponging channels doesn't seem like a good place for dolphins to hunt. Dodger needs to find, tear off, and balance a sponge on her rostrum to protect her skin from the rubble and from any poisonous-spined fish she might bump into by accident. She gropes around half blind.

25

This seems like a lot of trouble. Why bother?

Janet and Eric are at work on a project to analyze sand perch flesh. "We think sand perch may be extra-nutritious," Eric explains. "Their flesh may have more fat than the flesh of other fish commonly eaten by dolphins in Shark Bay."

Happily—from Dodger's point of view—sand perch are also not very bright. "When I flush them out of hiding, they skitter a few feet away," Eric says. "They just sit out in the open, looking sort of surprised."

The agile Dodger then drops her sponge and slurps her prey. Sometimes she even surfaces for a leisurely *poooff* before diving back down to seize the flustered perch.

Dodger makes it look easy. But consider the complex series of behaviors she had to learn.

1. Find sponge.
2. Tear off sponge.
3. Balance sponge on rostrum.
4. Swim to channel bottom.
5. Poke around bottom.
6. Drop sponge when tasty fish is uncovered.
7. Eat tasty fish.
8. Don't forget where sponge was dropped. Otherwise you waste time and energy repeating steps 1 and 2.

Inventing a specialized skill like sponging can be risky because innovation requires time and effort. If the innovation does pay off, however, having a special hunting skill can help an animal survive.

Dolphins don't have *Sponging for Dummies* reference books. Dodger must have learned her skills by closely watching her mother, since calves sponge only if their mom sponges. Dodger's mom learned by watching Dodger's grandmother . . . and back along the maternal line to the dolphin Janet calls "the first sponging Eve."

Perhaps sponging began as play. Imagine a young female dolphin who goofed around with a bit of sponge and idly poked here and there. A sand perch bolted; the dolphin's jaws snapped. This unexpected reward stuck in the dolphin's fertile mind. She tried it again. Perhaps the results were mixed, but she kept practicing. Her sponging grew more and more efficient. When this clever dolphin became a mother, those regular meals of sand perch may have helped her calf survive. A hobby became a way of life—a way of life passed through the generations.

When using his sponge pole, Eric managed to scare up a sand perch every nine minutes. Dodger probably works faster. The fish Eric found averaged six inches (twelve centimeters) long—not a big meal, but reliable. And non-sponging dolphins probably can't find them very easily.

"Females are the specialists and the innovators because they're under a lot of pressure to support their calves," Janet explains. "If you're a female dolphin who can develop a new way of making a living instead of competing with other dolphins, that's a big advantage."

The day after we watched Dodger's sponging demo, Janet guides the *Pomboo* toward Peron Point, a line of green-edged red cliffs sandwiched between layers of blue. Janet has documented fifty-four spongers in the eastern part of Shark Bay. Other scientists recently discovered a different group of spongers fifty miles (eighty kilometers) away, in the western half of the bay. Peron Point lies in between.

"We really wondered if sponging was independently invented by different bottlenose dolphin populations," Janet says. "Or do

Peron Point, looking south.

A Shark Bay dolphin goes airborne. Sometimes a leap like this is just for fun. Other times it's an attempt to dislodge a sea lamprey—a leechlike fish with a vampire lifestyle.

sponging dolphins live along the coast between here and there?"

We find a channel and follow it. Within minutes we spot a brand-new sponger—number fifty-five!

"This is a big thrill," Janet says, grinning. "I expect we'll eventually find spongers all along the coast, as long as we find channel habitat."

The Shark Bay Dolphin Project database contains information on nearly six hundred living bottlenose dolphins. Those fifty-five spongers are a small clan amid the larger dolphin community. But sponging isn't the only odd foraging method perfected by Shark Bay's female dolphins.

After taking photos of the new sponger's dorsal fin, we head off. Without warning, a gray missile launches out of the sea to our right. A dolphin arches impossibly high before slamming back into the sun-sparkled water. I've watched this move at SeaWorld, yet when a dolphin chooses its own wild orbit, it is somehow completely different.

Our jumper doesn't reappear. The *Pomboo* bucks and tilts as we travel on across the choppy vortex where the tidal flows from the two halves of the bay mix. We spot what looks like a gigantic floating potato. The dugong (a slow-swimming marine mammal similar to a manatee) raises its lumpy head to stare before dropping out of sight. Ten thousand dugongs—the largest population in the world—live in Shark Bay.

We're not searching for dugongs, though. We're looking for Reggae and the Beachers. That might sound like the name of a steel drum band, but it's actually a group of female dolphins with a crazy talent.

A few minutes later we see a cluster of fins. It's thirty-four-year-old Reggae and her calf Jamaica; Reggae's best friend, Rhythm, with her calf Beat; and Rhythm's grown daughter, Blues. With them is Chi, a female who likes to hang with the beach hunters but doesn't beach hunt herself. Blues and Chi stroke each other fondly with their pectoral fins. The whole group drifts idly at the surface.

"I guess they're all working on their tans," Janet jokes.

At last Reggae moves off. She cruises slowly along a beach rimmed in dry,

A tiger shark eating a dugong carcass. Shark Bay's tiger sharks range from four to fifteen feet (1.4 to 4.5 meters) in length. Shark populations are plummeting all over the world because of the demand for shark's fin soup in China. Shark Bay is one of the last places in the world with a healthy population of large sharks.

Chi cruises the shallows near Peron Point. Dolphins often rest at the surface, but their skin can't stay dry and exposed for long periods of time. A dolphin's sensitive skin can sunburn, blister, and peel.

dead sea grass that looks like shredded newspaper. Reggae's searching for small schools of fat mullet. The beach—a steep, sandy slope—is ideal for her hunting strategy. The angle decreases her chances of being stranded and makes the fish think they're safe in deep water. Until they aren't.

Reggae herds her victims closer and closer to the beach. Then, without warning, she makes her kamikaze run. Panicked mullet scatter. Some dart toward the beach; Reggae rockets after them, allowing her momentum to carry her completely out of the water. There's no escape for the mullet. Now, of course, Reggae is high and dry. She must scoot and shimmy, like someone trying to fit into snug jeans, back into the water.

Beach hunting is a dangerous method that requires a long apprenticeship. Year-old calves make runs at the shallows, but youngsters don't completely beach themselves until about age six. Even so, only daughters of beach hunters fully master the trick—probably because daughters stay with their mother longer than sons do. Spongers are rare; beach hunters such as Reggae are even rarer. Only six Shark Bay females make the daring slide from sea to sand.

As Reggae stalks a school of nervous mullet, Janet tells me about the time she was standing on the beach watching Reggae hunt. Reggae slammed into a fish and knocked it far out of the water. When the fish landed at Janet's feet, Janet tossed the mullet back.

"She chased it down again and ate it," Janet reports. "Reggae didn't miss a beat."

Shark Bay dolphins have other oddities. Some forage in shallow sea-grass beds by "kerplunking": making sharp tail slaps that

The beach-hunting dolphins have a long and skinny home range that runs along this remote beach. Janet once spent six weeks camped here to study beach hunting up close.

Reggae hydroplanes into the shallows in pursuit of a fish.

Gotcha! Reggae nabs a mullet as two other dolphins (dorsal fins just visible) watch from deeper water.

startle the fish into the open. One female hunts stingrays, a prey other Shark Bay dolphins rarely eat. Another dolphin sometimes steals fish from sea birds. "She finds a cormorant floating with a fish in its mouth and then slams into the cormorant," Janet says. "When the bird drops the fish, she grabs it."

Janet studied one female named Square. Square was a successful mom, but she didn't seem to do anything except snooze and socialize. On a hunch, Janet stayed out after dark on a calm, moonlit night. She tracked Square by listening for the dolphin's breaths.

"As soon as the sun went down, Square foraged for four hours straight," Janet says. "I think she's eating nocturnal prey, like squid."

Some Shark Bay dolphins also jiggle large shells at the surface. Apparently the dolphins chase a small fish into an empty shell, then bring the shell to the surface and shake it like a piñata. Eventually the water drains out. So does the fishy goodie.

The most incredible hunter in Shark Bay, however, is Janet's favorite dolphin, Wedges.

Twelve years ago Janet enrolled Wedges in her mother-

A trumpet shell gets a shakedown; the brown bit on the dolphin's chin is probably a chunk of broken shell. Shell-shaking seems to be spreading among dolphins of the same age rather than from mothers to calves.

calf study. Wedges had given birth in May, well outside the normal calving season, so Janet dubbed Wedges's baby Whoops. Janet knew Wedges but had never observed her for an extended time. The very first time Janet followed Wedges and Whoops, Wedges made a tail-up dive in deep water. A few seconds later she took off on a high-speed, leaping chase.

What was Wedges after?

Janet trailed Wedges in her boat. Little Whoops followed too. When Wedges brought up her catch, Janet couldn't quite believe it. A three-foot-long (one meter) golden trevally, a far bigger fish than anything Shark Bay dolphins normally eat, struggled in Wedges's jaws. Wedges dove deep—probably to snap the trevally's neck against the bottom. Afterward she carried her trophy into the shallows.

Wedges carries a large golden trevally.

Young calves usually nurse every ten minutes or so. Poor Whoops had to wait nearly an hour as Wedges tore up the trevally and ate it. The calf darted back and forth, whistling constantly, as if to say, *I'm here, Mommy! What about ME?*

The trevally's blood attracted two large tiger sharks and several smaller reef sharks. Wedges dashed out of the shallows to drive the sharks away, somehow managing to defend her catch and her calf without losing either.

Janet wondered if Wedges's big fish was just a big fluke. But Wedges did it again a few hours later. If Samu's baitfish are like eating sunflower seeds one at a time, and Dodger's sand perch are like eating french fries one at a time, then Wedges's trevally feasts are like wolfing down an extra-large pizza. Solo.

Once, after gorging on a particularly enormous trevally, Wedges swam into shallow water and lay unmoving for four hours. Janet thought she looked just like someone suffering a post-Thanksgiving stomachache.

Other Shark Bay dolphins treat Wedges like a celebrity. "When other dolphins see her with a trevally, they rush over to watch her eat," Janet reports.

And little Whoops isn't so little anymore. "At first Whoops screamed her head off while her mom was busy eating in shallow water, but she figured out how to nurse-nurse-nurse while Wedges carried her catch toward the shallows," Janet explains. "Most calves nurse for three or four years. Whoops nursed for eight. She's huge."

Twelve-year-old Whoops now hunts in a manner similar to her mother's, and she may be catching smaller golden trevally. "Whoops is probably pregnant now. When she has her own calf to support, I think she'll start going after the big ones," says Janet.

Sponging, kerplunking, midnight feeding, sea-bird slamming, shell shaking, beach hunting, and trevally catching: Why so many different strategies in one place, among one population of dolphins?

When small groups (such as the spongers or the beach hunters) or individual females (such as Wedges) specialize, they aren't competing directly with other dolphins for food. They are expanding into new territory and reaping the rewards. However, the rewards aren't won without effort. Reggae's and Wedges's techniques demand Olympian speed, strength, and coordination. These two moms are Shark Bay's ultimate athletes. Think Michael Jordan and Michael Phelps—except with kids in tow.

Many Shark Bay foraging methods also demand brainpower. Inventing a skill or learning a complex skill from Mom requires curiosity, long-term memory, mental flexibility, and the ability to solve problems.

Why are dolphins smart?

Perhaps you've heard the saying "Necessity is the mother of invention." Among dolphins, invention is sometimes a necessity of motherhood. Janet thinks that a mother dolphin's struggle to get the extra nutrition she needs to support her calf could be a factor in the evolution of dolphin

Pied cormorants watch Rhythm slide onto the beach. DNA tests revealed that Rhythm, Reggae, and the other beach hunters are related to some of Shark Bay's spongers.

intelligence. Clever moms probably eat better. Their calves survive more often than the calves of less clever females. Those calves inherit Mom's agile mind and body.

Yet food isn't the whole story. There's another factor, one that scientists think might have an even bigger influence on dolphin brainpower. To understand it, you need to know more about dolphin society. And where does a youngster learn his or her first social lessons?

On the playground, of course.

Cheeky and Lick ride the wave created by the *Pomboo's* bow. Bow riding allows Janet to identify dolphins, confirm their sex, and check their condition.

CHAPTER FOUR

YOUNG AND RESTLESS

The first fins appear just a few hundred yards from the Monkey Mia dock.

"Lick and Cheeky," Janet calls to Kipp Searles. "Begin survey at eleven twenty-five."

Kipp sits in the bow of the *Pomboo* with clipboard and survey form. She notes the names of the dolphins, the time, the GPS (Global Positioning System) location, the water depth and temperature. Kipp is learning from Janet the way Janet learned from Professor Altmann, the primatologist who developed a more accurate way of studying animal behavior.

At the moment, I'm Janet's newest student. She explains her two most important sampling methods: the survey and the focal follow.

"The survey is like a snapshot, and the focal follow is like a movie," Janet says. "Let's say I took a snapshot of you on random days. In one picture you're talking on your cell phone, in another you're sitting at your computer, in another you're eating lunch. I would know a little bit about you. But if I videotaped you for an entire day and noted how much time you spent eating, walking, reading, or whatever, and who you talked to, I would have a much better idea of what your life is like and who is in your social circle."

When Janet and her colleagues come across a group of dolphins, they often gather data using a quick five-minute survey. The survey's a snapshot. Which dolphins are present? What are they doing?

The mother dolphin's tail flips up. Her calf dives too.

Cheeky follows his mother, Lick, past kayakers.

All dolphins have a longer genital slit and a shorter anal slit on their underbellies. But females also have two small mammary slits on either side of the genital slit. The upside-down dolphin is male.

"Lick, TD foraging. Calf PD," Janet says to Kipp. TD is short for "tail-up dive." Lick is hunting for fish; her steep dive brings her tail flukes out of the water. PD is short for "peduncle dive." Cheeky is making a less steep dive in which only his peduncle—the area behind the dorsal fin—appears above water.

Moments later, the two resurface. Janet wants to get a closer look at Cheeky, so she drives the *Pomboo* at an enticing bow-riding speed. The slipstream created by a moving boat is a dolphin carnival ride.

Lick and Cheeky veer over to surf our bow wave. The mother dolphin turns sideways to gaze through the thin film of water. Janet has known Lick since Lick was just a calf herself. The twenty-six-year-old female has survived four shark attacks and raised another son and a daughter. Two-year-old Cheeky streaks along beside his mom. Odd dark marbling covers Cheeky's body. The calf wasn't born this way, so it must be a disease.

"The kid's got a terrible skin problem," Janet says, frowning. "No idea what it is."

Janet wants to know if Cheeky is male or female. Dolphins often bow ride upside down, giving researchers a handy glimpse of their under-bellies. But Cheeky doesn't flip over. The little dolphin's sex remains a secret.

When Lick and Cheeky glide away, Janet slows the *Pomboo* to a putter. "End survey, eleven thirty," Janet tells Kipp. "Begin focal follow."

Since Lick and Cheeky are part of Janet's ongoing mother-calf study, she wants to gather more detailed behavior data. End the snapshot. Cue the movie.

Janet sets her watch. For the next hour it will buzz every sixty seconds. At the buzzer, Janet calls out Lick's and Cheeky's behavior to Kipp. Because everything the dolphins do, minute by minute, is written down, the data are less likely to be biased by an observer choosing only the ac-tions that *seem* important. Each on-the-minute observation is a tiny sample of dolphin behavior.

Lick whisks through the water, turns, and darts in another direction. This technique is called mill foraging. Lick is feeding on a school of fish swimming near the surface. Like tail-up and peduncle-up diving, mill foraging is a common dolphin hunting method in Shark Bay. Dol-phins such as Dodger, Reggae, and Wedges are specialists; Lick is a generalist. A dolphin such as Lick may use as many as seven different hunting methods.

Buzz. Janet glances at her watch. "Mom is mill foraging, calf is . . ." She frowns. "Trying to get into BP."

BP stands for "baby position." Newborns swim above their mother, sort of perched on her shoulder (if dolphins had shoulders). Older calves usually travel in baby position, slightly below and behind their mothers. As soon as a mother begins foraging, however, her calf usu-ally moves off. Kids must entertain themselves when Mom's got work to do.

A Shark Bay calf swims in baby position, slightly below and behind its mother.

Tiger sharks are Shark Bay's top predators. Shark Bay Ecosystem Research Project scientists capture and release tiger sharks in order to learn more about them. Sometimes a captured shark vomits up its most recent meal, giving the scientists a handy (if unappetizing) way of analyzing what sharks eat. Shark Bay's tiger sharks mainly prey on dugongs, sea turtles, sea snakes, and fish.

Janet is worried about Cheeky. "When a calf is in poor condition, it stays in baby position more often," she explains.

How does Janet know?

As you may recall, 44 percent of all Shark Bay dolphin calves die before weaning. Survey data collected by Janet and other researchers document when a female known to have a calf is suddenly seen *without* her baby. If the calf doesn't reappear, it is presumed dead.

Janet wanted to know the main cause of calf death. She had two ideas: 1) calves were killed by sharks, or 2) calves were dying from starvation and/or disease.

Testing ideas scientifically requires forming a hypothesis, gathering data, and figuring out what the data mean. Janet's first hypothesis was *Bottlenose calf deaths in Shark Bay are mostly due to shark predation*. Janet's alternative hypothesis was *Bottlenose calf deaths in Shark Bay are mostly due to poor calf condition*.

How could Janet separate death by shark from death by other means? Shark Bay researchers had witnessed only a handful of shark attacks. But survey data could help. Tiger sharks live year round in Shark Bay, but the population increases during the Australian summer (January to April), when large tiger sharks migrate in from the Indian Ocean. If sharks are mainly responsible for calf deaths, then calf deaths per month should be higher during those months than at other times.

Surprisingly, the survey data didn't support Janet's shark hypothesis. Calves disappeared at about the same rate every month.

Shark Bay dolphins don't have any predators besides sharks. That means most calves must die because they're diseased, or not getting enough to eat, or both. (This doesn't mean that sharks never eat dolphin calves. Sharks may successfully attack calves weakened

When a calf like Samu is away from his mother, Puck, he can still track her by listening to her echolocation clicks. When Puck's clicks stop, Samu knows she is no longer hunting and he can go back to nurse.

The information Kipp writes on the focal-follow sheet will be added to the Shark Bay Dolphin Project computer database.

by disease or starvation, but it seems that sharks are killing calves that would die anyway.) Could Janet predict which calves were most likely to die?

She turned to her focal-follow data. Focal follows gave minute-by-minute details about each calf's behavior. She compared calves that eventually died with calves that survived and discovered that at-risk calves spent more time in baby position.

A sickly kid needs Mommy.

Playmates arrive for Cheeky: Puck's sons Samu and India.

Kipp notes the new dolphins on the focal-follow sheet. Janet's buzzer goes off.

"Mom mill for, calf soash," Janet says. Translation: Lick continues mill foraging while Cheeky socializes.

Brothers Samu and India swim in tandem, chasing Cheeky. "The calf in front is 'it,'" Janet explains. "The calf in front tries to swerve and get behind the dolphins chasing him."

Lick swims over. "She's checking on Cheeky," Janet says approvingly. "Lick's such a great mom."

Everybody's making nice, so Lick returns to hunting. Every now and then a sharp whistle pierces the air as the youngsters play. Underwater it must sound like a playground at recess.

Humans make noises in their throats using vocal cords. Dolphins make noises by sending air through a modified nostril near their blow-hole. The youngsters are probably making social whistles—the meaning of which is unknown. Every dolphin also has a "signature" whistle that it uses when separated from family or friends. Cheeky's signature whistle probably means something like *I'm Cheeky! I'm over here!*

As Cheeky, Samu, and India play, the positions in the dolphin triangle change. Now Samu's in front. India and Cheeky dart forward simultaneously to "goose" Samu—jabbing Samu's rear end with their rostrums. It's a dolphin-style prank.

Samu swims in front of India and Cheeky.

Seven-year-old India lifts his head and chin-slaps the water. Samu swerves behind his big brother. The two-year-olds, Samu and Cheeky, chase India.

"India's now 'it,'" Janet says. "They're taking turns. Very democratic!"

Brainy animals play. Brainy animals *need* to play. A shark gets along quite well with a smaller brain and simpler behavior, but more intelligent animals need to test themselves. Play—whether it's puppies wrestling, chimpanzees tickling, dolphins chasing, or human children pretending to be puppies or chimps or dolphins—develops skills. Some skills are physical. Some, such as taking turns, are social.

"When boys grow up, they form alliances with other males," Janet explains. "Male alliances herd females that are in estrus [ready for mating]."

The game Cheeky, Samu, and India are playing clearly imitates male herding. It's a warm-up for adulthood. Right now India plays the role of the herded female while Samu and Cheeky practice being herders. India manages to drop back; now Samu's "it" again. By taking turns, young dolphins develop trust. They're showing one another that they are the sorts of guys who can be team players. And yes . . . from the way Cheeky's playing, Janet thinks the calf is male.

This may be a playful little romp, but among adult dolphins, herding is serious business.

A female bottlenose can have only a limited number of calves during her lifetime. Each one is a big investment of time and energy. A female's best mating strategy is to choose the strongest, healthiest male to father her precious babies.

A male dolphin's strategy is quite different. Since the burden of raising calves falls entirely on the females, the best way for a male dolphin to spread his genes is to get as many females pregnant as possible. But each adult female comes into estrus once every four years or so. That means scores of males must compete for every mating opportunity. A Shark Bay female should get to choose the best male.

Ah, but wait. If you're a male dolphin, you don't want the female to choose, because the odds are against you. How do you take away a female's ability to choose? If you're a smart dolphin, you join up with your buddies. You turn pirate. The motto of male herding seems to be, *You'll not get away, wench. Mate with us . . . or nobody!*

A three-dolphin herding alliance is ideal: one male swims directly behind the female, and two swim on either side and slightly behind. You must share your captive with your partners, but a one-in-three chance of fatherhood is better than one in fifty.

This is a dolphin battle of the sexes. Prisoners are taken.

Good mother Puck arrives to check on little Samu. After deciding that all is well, she joins Lick to mill forage. Janet's not surprised to see Puck; the sociable female has a network of girlfriends all around Monkey Mia and Red Cliff Bay.

India, Samu, and Cheeky seem to tire of their herding game. The brothers join their mom while Cheeky returns to Lick.

"Cruising travel one," Janet calls out to Kipp. Translation: Lick and Cheeky travel slowly, about two to three miles per hour (three to five

kilometers per hour), and they are swimming between one to six and a half feet (thirty centimeters to two meters) apart.

The new arrivals are adult males: Cookie, Urchin, and Real Notch. The three belong to a larger male alliance dubbed the Red Cliff Rascals. Cookie is Real Notch's son and Puck's younger half brother.

Real Notch has his own history with Puck. He and two alliance partners once jealously herded Puck around the clock for a record-setting fifty-one days. A year later Puck gave birth to Piccolo. DNA tests showed that Real Notch is Piccolo's father. He also fathered Puck's other daughter, Kiya.

The three males hopscotch through the water in high, curving leaps. This behavior is called leap and porpoise foraging—a way of feeding on fast-moving fish that swim midway between the bottom and the surface. From their prey's perspective it's like being dive-bombed by a 747 jet.

Lick begins leap and porpoise foraging too, though she keeps her distance from Cookie, Urchin, and Real Notch. Puck and the three young dolphins also hang back. Females, calves, and juveniles usually won't join adult males. Not willingly, anyway.

After a few minutes the fishing seems to fizzle. Cookie, Urchin, and Real Notch depart.

Puck, Samu, and India gather to rest, hanging motionless in the water with only their blowholes showing. Humans breathe automatically, even while asleep. Dolphins don't. Every breath they take is a

43

conscious decision. So a dolphin rests in nano naps, shutting down half its brain for a few minutes while keeping the other half awake enough to breathe. Resting together gives dolphins some protection against sharks. A shark is less likely to attack a group. And more dolphins means a higher likelihood that one of the dolphins will notice an approaching predator. If an attack does happen, the flurry of fleeing bodies may confuse the shark.

Precautions don't always work. Three months earlier a large shark attacked India, leaving a jagged wound on his back. Dolphins instinctively twist their underside away from a shark's jaws because a bite on the dorsal fin or back is easier to survive than one to the belly. Still, it must have hurt terribly. Does India dream as he floats, half dozing, in the water? Does he suffer shark-attack nightmares?

Lick and Cheeky disappear underwater, probably to allow Cheeky to nurse. Lick surfaces and performs a graceful tail-up dive. She's off to forage for bottom-dwelling morsels. Instead of moving away a short distance to give his mother the space she needs, Cheeky sticks to Lick like a postage stamp.

Janet sighs. "That kid really has bad timing."

The big guys, from left to right: Cookie, Real Notch, and Urchin. Cookie is Puck's younger half-brother.

India's fresh shark bite, and the healed scar four months later. About three-fourths of all adult Shark Bay dolphins bear shark-bite scars, a proportion twice as high as that of bottlenose dolphins living in other places.

After a few minutes Lick gives up. Lick and Cheeky head toward the Monkey Mia dock.

Janet smiles. "Look . . . they're taking us home."

Shark Bay tests every wild bottlenose dolphin. *Can you catch enough food? Can you find mates and leave offspring? Can you avoid falling prey to sharks? Can your body fight off diseases?* The smartest, strongest, quickest dolphins are the ones most likely to pass all these rigorous tests.

Janet leans over the side of the *Pomboo* to take a closer look at Cheeky's markings. Maybe Cheeky's just an awkward kid. Maybe his problems are just skin-deep.

"I hope he makes it," she murmurs.

If Cheeky survives weaning, new challenges await. Dolphin adolescence is a time for wandering freely and developing the skills needed to succeed in dolphin society. Juvenile dolphins must find friends, uncover enemies, and put up with bullies. They must learn when to trust and when to fluke off into the sunset. In other words, a juvenile dolphin's world resembles middle school.

But with sharks.

Although dolphins are highly intelligent, most other animals have evolved ways of making a living that require little or no intelligence. The tiger shark is Shark Bay's top predator, yet tiger sharks have small brains. Diverse marine habitats provide a home for many species with different survival strategies.

Guppy swims past the *Pomboo*'s bow. Bottlenose dolphins such as Guppy are found in all tropical (warm) and temperate (neither warm nor cold) seas.

CHAPTER FIVE

DATING GAMES

"TD," Eric announces. Another day, another focal follow. Today nine-year-old Guppy is the object of Eric and Janet's attention.

They're interested in Guppy not because of what he does, but because of what he *doesn't* do.

Janet has watched several generations of sponging moms raise calves. Daughters of spongers always become spongers. But only about a quarter of sons take up sponging. Guppy is a son of a sponger, but he's never been seen sponging. Why not?

"Somebody coming, eleven o'clock," Eric says. Translation: Dolphins are arriving from a point just to the left of the *Pomboo*'s bow.

That tilted, notched fin—it's our sponging sweetie, Dodger. She's with another juvenile sponger, twelve-year-old Kooks. Guppy has known Dodger and Kooks since he was a baby.

"The three of them aren't related," Janet says, "but they all come from upstanding sponger families. Their moms are good friends."

Janet explains that juvenile dolphins spend much of their time getting to know their neighbors. "Like us, dolphins have big social networks. We have our family, who we spend most of our time with, but as we grow up, we have an ever-widening circle. We have friends, acquaintances, and those whose faces we recall but not their names."

Each Shark Bay dolphin has a home range that overlaps the home range of many other dolphins. Daughters usually stay within their mother's area. Sons wander a little bit farther, but sons' home waters always overlap a large portion of their mother's. Dolphin society is close-knit—yet as fluid as the sea.

Playful Dodger flips belly-up. Guppy and Kooks roll on top of her. This sort of play mimics adult mating behavior; it prepares the three juveniles for adulthood. Older dolphins have serious responsibilities. Males must pay attention to alliance partners, and females must pay attention to their calves. Juveniles get to practice grown-up roles without taking it too seriously. This isn't the Big Game; it's just the tryouts.

Eleven-year-old Dodger is near sexual maturity. Most Shark Bay females become fertile around age twelve, so next year Dodger will probably be captured and herded by a male alliance. Nine-year-old Guppy won't get a chance to breed until age fourteen or older. Males must mature socially as well as physically in order to join an existing male alliance or form one of their own. If he's lucky, Guppy will find guys he can trust.

Playful Dodger leaps out of the water.

Guppy and Kooks swim behind Dodger in the typical position of males herding a female. Sometimes they dart forward to mount in sync, sandwiching Dodger between them. Sometimes they roll onto her one by one.

Is Kooks male or female? Kooks hasn't flipped over during a bow ride, so nobody's identified the dolphin's sex. From the masculine way Kooks acts, though, Janet thinks Kooks is male.

"Although you never know," she says, smiling. "Nothing dolphins do surprises me."

Buzz goes Janet's watch.

"Guppy and Kooks behind Dodger," Eric says.

"Kooks and Guppy mount Dodger," adds Janet.

Buzz.

Guppy, Dodger, and Kooks practice mating behavior.

"Kooks and Guppy charge Dodger." Turning to me, Janet says, "They can play like this for hours."

Janet explains that an older female wouldn't put up with this much friskiness from juvenile males (assuming Kooks is male), but Dodger is still young. Juvenile males clearly benefit from this kind of play because they need to test their herding skills and their bonds with other young males. It's not as clear how playing dating games helps a young female.

Janet says that sometimes young females swim in front of males, as if asking to be herded. "Adult females never do that," Janet explains, "but juveniles can be real flirts."

When Dodger comes into estrus—probably in a year or so—she won't have any choice about which male alliance herds her. But she *may* have some choice among her captors. Will it be male number one, male number two, or male number three? Practice with Guppy and Kooks may help Dodger figure out how to escape a herding alliance or avoid the attentions of one male in favor of another. Like the other juveniles, she's learning what her big brain can do for her.

Dolphins didn't always have big brains. They weren't even always dolphins.

Fifty-two million years ago, a mammal lived near ancient waterways. Though it looked vaguely wolfish, it wasn't a wolf. Scientists think that some of these wolfish-looking creatures began hunting fish in the shallows. Over time, the ones that could swim better ate better. They were able to raise more offspring than the ones that kept their paws dry.

Evolution works mainly through something called natural selection. All creatures, even members of the same species, vary slightly from one another. Some of these small, random differences—shorter legs, a stronger tail, nostrils set a bit higher—may help an animal survive and reproduce. If so, the variation will be passed to future generations. Sometimes the differences aren't only how an animal looks, but how it behaves.

Small variations. The environment tests; the environment selects. Many small variations over many generations can add up to big changes. This is how evolution reshapes the world.

An artist's re-creation of extinct _Ambulocetus natans_, the prehistoric ancestor of modern whales and dolphins.

After five million years those early wolfish-looking mammals evolved into a creature called *Ambulocetus natans* (am-byu-lo-SEE-tus na-TANS), which means "walking whale." Modern-day whales and dolphins are beautiful, but their ancestor *Ambulocetus* looked like a cross between a crocodile and a pit bull.

Generation by generation, their watery environment shaped *Ambulocetus*'s descendants. Dull hearing sharpened into sophisticated sonar. Front feet became paddle-shaped fins, and back feet disappeared. The tail stretched, flattened, and divided into a fluke. Nostrils moved up and back. One nostril turned into the blowhole; the other changed into the "phonic lip" that allows dolphins to whistle. And cetacean ancestors didn't simply become sleek and sassy. Their brains grew bigger too. Oversize brains are costly because brain cells burn much more energy than other types of cells. A big brain must deliver significant survival advantages to offset this disadvantage; as a result, only a few species have wandered down this evolutionary path. Both humans and dolphins are biological oddballs.

Guppy breaks away from Kooks and Dodger. Apparently he's worked up an appetite. He makes a steep dive; a floating cormorant nearby rolls underwater, almost in sync with Guppy. Dolphins and cormorants have an interesting relationship. Sometimes cormorants take advantage of prey scared up by foraging dolphins. In turn, dolphins sometimes stick their heads out of the water to look for cormorants diving into schools of fish. Then they rush over to grab a piece of the action. And sometimes dolphins goose floating cormorants . . . just for fun.

Dodger swims over to the *Pomboo*. "Hi, Dodgie!" Janet says.

Dodger dives and resurfaces with a knobby sponge. Down she goes again. Eric the human sponger thinks Dodger could improve her technique.

"Instead of picking up a sponge, scaring a fish, dropping the sponge, and repeating it all," Eric points out helpfully, "she could flush several fish. *Then* drop her sponge."

"Put that in the dolphin suggestion box," Janet replies.

Kooks pops up wearing a basket sponge. Guppy and Kooks begin diving side by side.

Janet wonders if Guppy is eating the prey Kooks is flushing. "Is he taking advantage of Kooks?"

"Another dolphin joining." Eric points. "That's Rang."

A few days earlier we had watched five-year-old Rang frolic with an

Guppy (on left) and his pal Kooks.

Dodger takes a break from playing with Guppy and Kooks.

older female. Rang seemed entranced. He twirled, spy hopped, and leaped. Rang even brought a bouquet to his crush (okay, it was a blade of sea grass). The female flipped belly-up and let Rang swim close behind. Then she whacked him on the head, one-two-three, with her tail flukes.

So now we have Dodger, Kooks, Guppy, and Rang. All offspring of sponging moms. Female Dodger sponges. Kooks—who is probably male—also sponges. Guppy is a male who has never been seen with a sponge. Rang sponged as a young calf but now doesn't sponge at all. Why does sponging seem difficult for males? Are boys less smart?

Janet doesn't think so. She thinks sons of spongers are less likely to take up the family trade than daughters because of the demands of male social life.

Sponging is a slow, steady job. Long hours spent in deep channel habitats leaves less time for socializing. This lifestyle works fine for female dolphins. However, the need to form strong alliances with other guys dominates a male dolphin's life. If you must spend a lot of time sponge foraging, it's best if your alliance partner sponges too.

"I think Guppy doesn't sponge because he just doesn't have enough sponge buddies," Janet says.

Rang, who is four years younger than Guppy, faces the same problem. That may be why Rang stopped sponging. Kooks—the (maybe) male who does sponge—seems like the wildcard.

Testing Janet's hypothesis will require gathering detailed data on Guppy, Rang, and other sons of spongers over many years. Who do sons of spongers socialize with as calves and juveniles? Who do they ally with as adults? What foraging method do they ultimately use?

Dodger, Guppy, Kooks, and Rang are all tail-up foraging as a rolling pair of fins draws near. Who's arriving?

I decide to try a fin ID. Six days on the *Pomboo*, a pair of binoculars around my neck, and I'm practically a scientist. Right?

Luckily, the *Pomboo* carries cheat sheets: photos of dozens of dorsal fins labeled with dolphin names and birth years. I flip through laminated pages. Clearly, Shark Bay dolphins get named by people who spend many hours in a small boat with only an apple between them and dinner. There are animals named Cookie, Taffy, Candy, Hershey, Godiva, Cocoa, Pasta, Pimento, Fondue, Tasty, Bread, Butter, Pumpernickel, Tamale, Chili, and Enchilada.

Now I'm hungry too. Can we name the next calf Saliva?

Before I can offer this excellent suggestion, Janet calls out, "It's Barney and Ridges."

Dodger immediately disappears. Apparently, flirting with Barney and Ridges isn't appealing. Moments later another male joins: Bigmidbite. Barney, Ridges, and Bigmidbite are all in their thirties. They belong to a larger alliance of seven males known as the Prima Donnas. If these guys wore clothing, their matching T-shirts might read:

The Prima Donnas
Pirating Shark Bay Females Since 1990!

The three adults mingle with the three youngsters. Five-year-old Rang, in particular, looks babyish next to the big dudes.

Janet, the former primatologist, explains that scientists often compare bottlenose dolphins with chimpanzees. Both are highly intelligent, highly social species. Yet dolphins face greater challenges. "Young chimps live in a group, but the group doesn't change much," she says. "Dolphin society changes so fast, it would make a chimp's head spin."

Why does a dolphin need so much brainpower?

Scientists think intelligence helps dolphins navigate their challenging social world. And right now Guppy, Kooks, and Rang face a challenge in the form of three hulking Prima Donnas.

Barney swims up behind Kooks and mounts, as if he's trying to mate. In dolphins this behavior isn't necessarily about reproduction. Sometimes it expresses playfulness or a social bond. Sometimes it says, *I'm the boss.*

Kooks escapes, scooting over to wedge between Guppy and Rang. The three youngsters crowd close as the Prima Donnas swim slowly behind. Guppy, Kooks, and Rang are "it" in a herding game they don't want to play. The trio look like skinny teenagers who wandered into a dark alley.

Things happen aboard the *Pomboo* that don't go into the database. Like the unscientific (yet irresistible) urge to say aloud what the dolphins might be thinking.

"*Uh-oh,*" says Jenny.

"*I think we're in trouble,*" mimics Janet.

"*We'll be okay if we all stick together,*" adds Eric.

As the Prima Donnas glide into goosing range, Guppy, Kooks, and Rang suddenly seem to hear their mommies calling. They sprint away. Barney, Ridges, and Bigmidbite let them go.

Aboard the *Pomboo*, we can't help but laugh. How do the Prima Donnas react?

Dolphins make a whole orchestra of sounds, many above the range of human hearing. No one knows what, if anything, most of their sounds mean. But maybe—just maybe—one translates into *heh heh heh.*

Guppy and pals at play.

Bigmidbite moves in.

The older and younger dolphins mingle. All highly intelligent mammals (such as humans, chimpanzees, elephants, and dolphins) have complex social worlds. The same is true for brainy birds such as crows and parrots.

Shark Bay bottlenose dolphins are relatively small because they eat small prey. Adults are only 6.5 feet (two meters) long and about 290 pounds (130 kilograms). However, bottlenose dolphins living off northern Europe eat larger prey. They grow to more than 13 feet (4 meters) in length and weigh more than 400 pounds (200 kilograms).

CHAPTER SIX

ADVANCED DOLPHINOMICS

On a fresh, clear morning we head toward Red Cliff Bay, swaying with the *Pomboo*'s rocking-horse gait. Eric spies a dolphin foraging. The animal doesn't stick around, but we find a whiting (a schooling fish) wobbling at the surface. Eric uses a milk crate to scoop it out.

"Dolphin tooth marks," he says, examining the punctures on the fish's silvery sides.

He slips it back into the water, but the fish is clearly too injured to survive. A predator or scavenger may nab it even before it sinks to the bottom.

A few minutes later we spot fins. "Begin survey at eight fifty a.m.," Janet tells Jenny.

An elderly female, Blip, is being herded by three Prima Donnas—Ridges, Bigmidbite, and Fred. Janet explains that this is a "consortship," a low-level off-season herding. The real breeding season won't begin for another three months. "This isn't the right time of year," Janet says. "Nobody's getting pregnant."

By September, however, females will begin coming into estrus. Nobody knows how the dolphins can tell, but males may use echolocation to assess a female's fertility.

Sometimes females don't seem to mind being herded. More often they resist. If a female tries to veer away, a male may make a low-frequency *pop* that means, *Stay close . . . or else!* If the female doesn't turn toward the popper, he may nip her. Sometimes angry males bombard a female with sound—cetacean shouting. If a female dares a serious escape, she may be chased down and punished with bites, ramming, tail whacks, or body slams. The guys can get rough.

Today, however, everybody's relaxed. Just a little preseason practice.

"More dolphins arriving," Eric announces.

It's three young females: Woof, Rhombus (daughter of Square, the night-hunting dolphin), and Eden (daughter of Piccolo, granddaughter of Puck and Real Notch). Eden bears tooth rakes on her side from an aggressive male. The three girls surround Blip.

"When males harass a female, sometimes other females will come and swim in sync with the one being picked on," Janet explains. "It's a sign of solidarity."

Woof, Rhombus, and Eden seem to be saying, *We're here to help.* Male social scheming tends to be more obvious and focuses on male alliances. Janet thinks that female social scheming centers on countermeasures to male herding. It's subtler and less well understood than male behavior, but probably just as savvy. (Remember those snarling male baboons and quietly grooming females?)

Janet tells me a remarkable story about Puck. Once, Puck was being herded by three males; one was Real Notch. Puck sought escape from Real Notch and his crew by darting into the midst of an

Eden (closest) with Rhombus (middle) and Blip.

Eric examines the injured whiting. Shark Bay dolphins eat whiting and at least thirty other species of fish.

all-girl gathering. When the guys approached to reclaim Puck, they were surrounded by a flurry of fawning females. The ladies stroked and petted Real Notch and his buddies. Meanwhile, two other females sandwiched Puck between them and sneaked away.

Once she was at a safe distance, Puck bolted. Her escorts swam casually back to join the fan club. A few moments later Real Notch and his partners suddenly seemed to realize they'd been duped. The males sped off in three different directions—but couldn't find Puck.

No *Mission Impossible* today. The dolphin sisterhood ignores the trailing males. Blip, Rhombus, Woof, and Eden rub and pet one another with their pectoral fins.

"Males don't like it when females bond," Janet notes. "Sometimes they'll push between them."

Ridges, Bigmidbite, and Fred's response to this female fest appears to be a call for reinforcement. Sound travels farther in water than in air; dolphins separated by more than a mile (several kilometers) can hear each other's whistles. And a dolphin as far as 200 yards (182 meters) away may be able to eavesdrop on the echoes from another dolphin's echolocation clicks—essentially "seeing" what a distant dolphin is seeing.

Whether by way of whistle or click or chance, Barney arrives. Now four Prima Donnas follow four females.

Janet's colleague, Richard Connor, has studied Shark Bay's male dolphins since the late 1980s. His research has revealed a fiendishly complex male society. Male dolphins often join an alliance of two other males to capture and herd a female. This is a "first-order alliance." And that's just the beginning. First-order alliances often mingle to form second-order alliances of six to fourteen males. The members of a second-order alliance will help one another steal females from rival alliances, or help defend their females from raiders. The seas are full of pirates looking for treasure.

Believe it or not, male dolphin politics can get even *more* complicated. The Prima Donnas are a second-order alliance. Shark Bay is home to many other second-order alliances, including the Red Cliff Rascals, the Punks, the Usual Suspects, the Blues Brothers, the Sharkies, the Wow

Eden pets a girlfriend.

Crowd, Hook's Crew, the Genghis Khans, the Krocker Spaniels, and the Dead Rockers.

There may even be *third-order* alliances in Shark Bay. For example, researchers have witnessed the second-order Prima Donnas and Krocker Spaniels apparently creating a third-order alliance to attack the Wow Crowd.

Shark Bay male dolphins are the only known animals, besides humans, that form second-order, and possibly third-order, alliances. Chimpanzees also form first-order alliances, but nothing more complicated. These dolphin alliances of alliances of alliances would definitely make a chimp's head spin. In fact, *my* head is spinning.

What's special about Shark Bay?

It might be the rich marine environment. Dolphin density is higher in Shark Bay than elsewhere because the fishing is good. More dolphins in a smaller area means that dolphins cross paths often, which means more opportunities for both competition and cooperation.

Two of the young females—Eden and Woof—suddenly leave. It's soon obvious why.

Dolphins leap as the Prima Donnas and the females mingle.

"Cookie, Smokey, Urchin," says Eric.

"Plus Lando and Real Notch," Janet adds. These five males belong to the Red Cliff Rascals, archrivals of the Prima Donnas. "Things are about to get really interesting."

Janet points out two of the approaching dolphins. "Cookie and Smokey have an unusual story," she says. "I'm really fond of Smokey. That's him . . . the one with the messed-up dorsal."

Smokey's mangled dorsal fin marks him as a shark-attack survivor.

Poor Smokey. Many dorsal fins in Shark Bay are marked with nicks and cuts, but Smokey's looks as if it went for a whirl in a garbage disposal. The twenty-three-year-old male has survived at least five shark attacks.

Smokey's life started well. He had a doting mother and a best friend, Cookie. When they were three years old and just weaned, both of their mothers died. Although Cookie stuck close to big sister Puck, he disliked the Monkey Mia beach scene and didn't want fish handouts from humans. He latched on to his longtime buddy and fellow orphan, Smokey. For four years Smokey and Cookie were inseparable. "Those two had the tightest bond ever between calves," Janet recalls.

In the normal course of events, the pair would have stuck together. The boys would have kissed up to older ladies, gotten scared by older guys, and played herding and mating games with other adolescents. Around age fourteen Cookie and Smokey would have turned pro. They would have found a third buddy, formed a first-order alliance, and conspired with other alliances. Cookie and Smokey might have stayed together forever.

But one day when Cookie and Smokey were seven years old, Smokey disappeared. Cookie was seen swimming alone or with another young male named Urchin.

Uh-oh. What had happened to Smokey?

Several days passed. Cookie joined Jesse, another young male. Janet assumed that Smokey was dead—most likely killed by a shark. She mourned the plucky little fellow.

Four days later Smokey reappeared . . . minus a few chunks of flesh. When Smokey tried to rejoin his best friend, Cookie acted as if Smokey's shark wounds were contagious. Whenever Smokey came near, Cookie and Jesse swam away.

Cookie spent the next few years shunning Smokey and building his own crew, which included his new buddies Jesse and Urchin. Meanwhile, Smokey became friends with Lando. Over time, Cookie's crew allied with Smokey, Lando, and Real Notch (Cookie's father) to become the Red Cliff Rascals.

Fred and his wingmen: Ridges (closest to camera) and Bigmidbite.

A male bottlenose dolphin must navigate a complex social world of friends, rivals, and rival friends. Remembering who helped you and who didn't is important. Does Smokey remember what Cookie did?

Janet certainly does. "I think Cookie pushed Smokey in front of that shark," she says.

Janet's joking, of course. Yet scientists often have seesaw emotions about the animals they get to know. A scientist strives to be objective, but it is impossible not to have feelings about Cookie's treatment of Smokey. Of course, Cookie's a dolphin and shouldn't be judged by human standards. Still . . .

To her credit, Janet doesn't want to say it. So I will.

Cookie is a jerk.

After Woof and Eden's hasty departure, Blip and her staunch friend, Rhombus, swim side by side. "The other two females left because all these males were too much for them," Janet explains. "It's really brave of Rhombus to stay."

The four Prima Donnas (Ridges, Bigmidbite, Fred, and Barney) follow the two females. Trailing the Prima Donnas are five members of the Red Cliff Rascals (Cookie, Urchin, Smokey, Lando, and Real Notch). The other four Rascals (there are nine in total), and the other three Prima Donnas (seven in total) are probably off foraging.

The Prima Donnas rise to breathe in unison; so do the Rascals. A baby dolphin grows up swimming in sync with its mom in order to stay close. In older dolphins this mirror swimming is a social statement.

We are united!

Male alliance members often move in perfect tandem. When herding a female, allied males may perform complex leaps, curves, and sprints, sometimes in opposite directions but always in unison. Humans also use synchrony. Think of school cheers at a football game, a class reciting the Pledge of Allegiance, or soldiers marching in step.

We are united!

As a first-order alliance develops among male dolphins, each may gradually change his unique signature whistle. A new signature—an alliance signature—is created and used by all the dolphins in the alliance. Like tandem jumps, this vocal tattoo probably advertises the tightness of the partnership's bond.

We are united!

Maybe this unity business helps a dolphin overlook how badly another dolphin in his alliance treated him when they were young. I'm not naming any names.

Janet watches the lineup of females, Prima Donnas, and Rascals. "The Rascals are trying to decide if it's worth a rumble."

Jenny laughs. "All this over Blip? She's an old lady!"

Blip and Rhombus pet each other with their pectoral fins as they swim. Within the Rascal troop, Urchin and Smokey are also petting. This coziness ends when a fountain of water erupts in the middle of the dolphin parade.

"Charge!"

"Tail whack!"

"Sync charge, Smokey and Lando!"

Eric and Janet call out the action as the males stir the water with charges and sharp, agitated turns. Most of it is bluff and bluster.

The rumble ends as abruptly as it began. Dolphins from both second-order alliances are petting and diving in sync with their alliance partners. It's as if they're backslapping and assuring each other: *Yeah, sure, we beat those guys!*

The action wasn't all bluff: fresh red scratches mark Cookie's dorsal fin. He departs with Urchin and Smokey.

Eric laughs. "Are they going off to make a master plan?"

The Prima Donnas drift toward Blip. Surprisingly, Rhombus swims over to Real Notch and pets him with her pectoral fin.

"Interesting," Janet muses.

When I ask why, she replies, "Real Notch is Rhombus's dad."

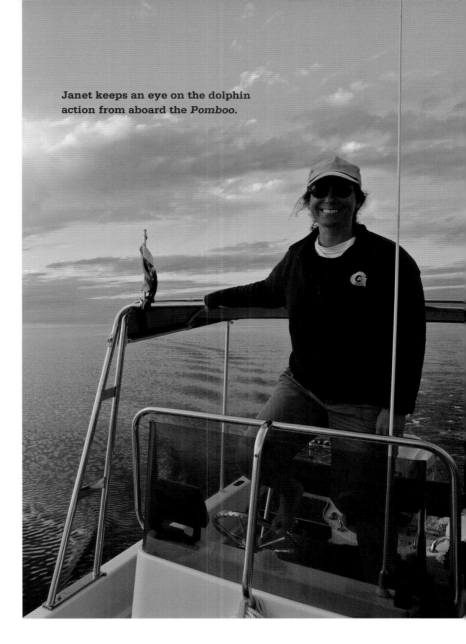

Janet keeps an eye on the dolphin action from aboard the *Pomboo.*

When Janet first met Real Notch, he was a teenager just beginning his career. Now Real Notch is something of a legend. This dolphin is very, very good at male-alliance politics. Which means he's also very, very good at spreading his genes. DNA studies conducted a few years ago show that Real Notch has at least six offspring—and probably many more. His son Cookie and daughter Rhombus are here today.

Real Notch started off with a close buddy. Over the next dozen years he lost his original partner, joined a new duo, joined a trio, and re-formed another trio. Sometimes two males in a three-dolphin alliance will act as if they barely tolerate the third. Although he allied with a total of ten other males, Real Notch was never the odd man out. The crafty pirate managed to become the captain of every crew.

Eventually Real Notch's partners died of old age. His glory days should have ended, but Real Notch refused to retire. Weaseling into the Prima Donnas was the obvious move. They were all close in age to Real Notch, and in those days he was friendly with them. Instead, Real Notch turned his considerable charms on the much younger Red Cliff Rascals. The old man's new allies, which include his son Cookie, are all strong guys in their prime. Real Notch is now around forty years old (no one knows his exact age); against all odds he's still in the game.

Three Red Cliff Rascals (Urchin, Cookie, and Real Notch) are flanked by three Prima Donnas (Bidmidbite, background; Fred, foreground; and an unidentified Prima Donna underwater).

Why do dolphins need a big brain?

Consider Real Notch's universe. He must pick first-order alliance partners. *Barney and Ridges, or Lando and Smokey? Who's dependable? Who's not?* He must have a memory for individuals and their past encounters. Choosing the wrong pals (or the wrong enemies) could cost him access to females.

Real Notch must also decide which larger group (the second-order alliance) to ally with. If Real Notch and his partners are herding a female and a group of rivals tries to steal her, he and his partners may need help from others in their second-order alliance to fight the raiders off. *Who will stand by me? Who won't?*

Interestingly, when one first-order alliance helps another steal or guard a female, the "helpers" don't mate with the female. The original alliance keeps those rights. Instead, when male dolphins assist each other, they are trading favors. Keeping track of favors owed and received demands brainpower.

Real Notch (closest), Cookie (with fresh tooth scrapes on his dorsal fin), and Urchin. Dolphins certainly know their mother and maternal siblings, but no one knows if fathers and their offspring—like Real Notch and Cookie—can recognize that they are related.

If Cookie and Urchin want me to help them steal Blip from the Prima Donnas, should I do it? Have they done anything for ME lately?

With so many ruthless, sharp-witted pirates around, things can change quickly. Partners are recruited or ousted; loyalties shift. Real Notch must constantly rethink his strategy if he wants to stay on top. *Hmmm, will Smokey be my friend forever if I shove COOKIE in front of a shark?*

Okay, maybe the scheming doesn't go *that* far. But if it does, Real Notch will probably end up on top.

At least until the ladies outsmart *him*.

Dodger surfaces with a sponge.

CHAPTER SEVEN

STICKY QUESTIONS

On a drizzly afternoon Janet and I depart on the *Pomboo*. Eric, Katie, Jenny, and Kipp stay behind to catch up on laundry and e-mail. We find Dodger sponging. Janet shuts off the engine and lets the *Pomboo* drift. Luckily for us, the rain clouds are moving inland to dampen the local kangaroos.

The salted air is soft and still. For once, no buzzers, no rapid-fire alphabet soup of TDs, PDs, and BPs. The *Pomboo* rocks to a silent lullaby. Dodger the dolphin surfaces and breathes—*poooff*—below a newly cast rainbow. The only thing missing from this dreamy picture is a unicorn.

Instead of discussing dolphins, Janet and I talk about Kenya. She tells me how she took time off after studying baboons and traveled to Lamu, an island off the Kenyan coast. Lamu's Swahili culture fascinated her. The Swahili lived in plastered houses with intricately carved wooden doors. They ate pickled limes and curried fish. The women covered themselves head to toe in black cloth. Janet's friendships with Swahili women helped her see her own culture in a new light.

Human culture, whether in New York or Lamu, consists of traditions passed down from one generation to another. Dodger also has a tradition—the sponging she learned from her mom, who learned it from Dodger's grandmother. Now Janet and other scientists are asking an intriguingly sticky question: Does this mean that dolphins have culture?

Dodger sponges as a rainbow lights up the landscape near Monkey Mia.

Captive dolphins have shown us that dolphins are smart. Thanks to the wild dolphins of Shark Bay, we have some idea *why* dolphins are smart. Intelligence helps a dolphin solve problems. *How can I support my calf?* Or: *How can I capture a female?*

Bottlenose dolphins have fertile minds; dolphins in different places come up with different solutions to their problems. Only Shark Bay dolphins are known to use sponge tools, even though sponges are found in other places where bottlenose dolphins live. And other dolphin populations have their own ingenious ways. Bottlenose dolphins in Florida trap schools of fish by stirring the shallows with their tails to create "mud rings"; the dolphins wait outside the ring and snap up the fish that try to jump out. Shark Bay dolphins don't do this. Do dolphins in Florida and Shark Bay have distinct local cultures?

"To show culture in animals," Janet says, "you need a definition of culture. And you need evidence."

Defining culture is difficult. Do local traditions equal culture? Or is culture something more? Does it require language? Or a moral code?

Scientists like to argue. In the argument over animal culture, anthropologists (scientists who study human societies) tend to think that humans are special. They point out that animals innovate but don't build on innovation. Dolphins use sponge tools, sure. But you don't see dolphins taking the tool idea and going further—for example, using dead branching coral as a rake that would last longer and cover a wider area. Human traditions get more complex over time, say the anthropologists, yet animal traditions don't. Most anthropologists insist that only humans have culture.

Biologists point out that humans have a long evolutionary history in common with other primates. It shouldn't be surprising to find glimmers of culture among our primate relatives. And although dolphins and whales aren't closely related to us, they are smart and sociable. Just like humans.

In fact, scientists *have* discovered a number of primate and cetacean traditions that might be labeled "cultural." Some involve tools, some involve prey capture, and some involve communication.

Chimpanzees living in different areas have distinct ways of cracking nuts with rocks. Some killer whales in South America beach themselves to snatch seal pups, and mothers show this unique behavior to their calves. Male humpback whales sing long, complex songs that conform to a local style. These songs also change over time, just as any song might if passed from one individual to another.

A few animal traditions are just plain quirky. Some groups of chimpanzees clasp hands overhead while grooming. Some Costa Rican capuchin monkeys stick their fingers in each other's nostrils, possibly to express trust. Neighboring monkeys don't.

Shark Bay's sponging dolphins may offer some of the best evidence yet for animal culture. Many Shark Bay dolphins visit the sponging channels to hunt for fish, but they simply chase whatever edible fish they see rather than sponging. So sponging isn't something that every dolphin will figure out just because it lives in the right habitat and the right tool is handy (or, from the dolphin's point of view, rostrum-y).

Could sponging be genetic—"hard-wired" into the

The culture of dolphin researchers (clockwise from the top: Katie, Janet, Eric, Kipp, and Jenny) includes gathering for meals in a leaky trailer that serves as kitchen, bunkhouse, and office.

Dolphin foraging methods like snacking, mill foraging, and porpoise foraging are commonly seen in bottlenose dolphin communities all over the world. Foraging methods like sponging and beach-hunting are extremely rare, even though sponges and beaches are found in many dolphin habitats.

brains of some dolphins? If so, it should spread the way a genetic trait spreads. But it doesn't. Instead, sponging spreads from mother to daughter (and sometimes from mother to son) the way a *learned* behavior does.

No one is sure exactly how calves learn sponging, but dolphins naturally imitate other dolphins. Remember all that synchrony? Perhaps junior spongers learn through trial and error mixed with mimicry.

In Janet's opinion, a scientific definition of culture should be broad enough to include nonhuman animals. "I think the right definition of culture is a socially learned behavior," she says. "Something that binds individuals together."

Janet suspected that spongers might have their own cultural identity. Do tool users see themselves as different from other Shark Bay dolphins? If so, how might this show up in the data?

Think of spongers as members of a soccer team. The team plays soccer, sure. But if you want to know whether teammates really have a strong team identity, look at them *off* the field. Do they walk around together? Do they do homework together? Do they go to the movies together?

The Shark Bay Dolphin Project surveys show which dolphins are usually seen together. Of course, you'd expect a dolphin to spend more time with neighboring dolphins than non-neighbor dolphins, more time with close relatives than nonrelatives, and more time with dolphins of the same sex than dolphins of the opposite sex (aside from herding). Statistical analysis can control (cancel out) these factors. What's left over can then be examined.

Sure enough, Janet's data suggest that spongers prefer other members of Team Sponge. It's as if everybody is wearing color-coordinated jerseys.

Which begs the question: What do tool users do when they hang out with other tool users?

"Well," says Janet, "I'm sure they check out each other's sponges."

Not surprisingly, people often want to talk to Janet about dolphins. Mostly Janet gets questions like these: Do dolphins save drowning

Each Shark Bay dolphin is familiar with sixty to seventy other dolphins, and probably recognizes many more. Their fission-fusion society gives dolphins a wide choice of friends.

people? (Probably not.) Do dolphins protect swimmers from sharks? (Probably not.) Is it possible to communicate with dolphins? (Depends on what you mean by "communicate.") And people want to talk about petting dolphins. Swimming with dolphins. Watching dolphins put on a show.

Janet thinks this misses the point. "The dolphins' interactions with each other," she says, "are far richer, more complex, and more interesting than any interactions they have with us."

Thanks in large part to studies of the dolphins of Shark Bay, we now better understand the richness and complexity of their lives in the wild. So here comes another sticky question.

Should we keep dolphins in captivity?

Consider Dodger. She swims freely though a varied habitat full of sea grass and sand flats, channels and banks, corals and nooks and crannies. Her world abounds with cormorants and sea turtles, dugongs and tiger sharks, poisonous fish and tasty fish. During the course of a day, Dodger may interact with dozens of other dolphins and listen to the whistles and clicks of many more. Her environment constantly tests her mind and body. Dodger's choices determine her survival.

Dolphins in captivity are sometimes (not always) well cared for. Yet no number of basketball hoops and belly rubs, no multimillion-gallon concrete tank, can possibly equal the free-ranging, fast-paced, challenging world that is the birthright of every wild-born dolphin.

The captivity question is complicated. Is it okay to keep dolphins in public aquariums and swim-with-the-dolphins programs because it's educational (for humans)? Is it okay to keep dolphins for research? Is it okay to capture wild dolphins for use in education or research? What about dolphins born in captivity? After all, captive-born dolphins probably couldn't survive in the wild. But . . . is it okay to breed dolphins that will never know a natural life?

Some of these questions may feel uncomfortable. That's not necessarily a bad thing. If the answer is easy, then it wasn't much of a question.

It's my last day in Shark Bay, my final trip on the *Pomboo*. As we leave the dock we catch sight of marble-skinned Cheeky and his mom, Lick. Puck cruises by with sons India and Samu while a trio of Red Cliff Rascals forage in the distance.

We keep going. Several minutes later, a small, perfect dorsal breaks the water next to a wickedly mangled fin. It's three-year-old Google and his sponger mother, Bytefluke, who is at least thirty-six years old. Bytefluke's long, heavy *pooooooff* sounds terribly weary.

Google zigzags around with youthful energy. Though Mom sponges, Google hasn't yet been seen with a sponge tool. A few days earlier, though, Janet did a focal follow of Bytefluke and Google. The calf disappeared for forty minutes.

"Maybe when he left, he was looking for sponges and doing some practice foraging," Janet muses. "It would be really exciting to see Google with a sponge today."

A cormorant startles us by dive-bombing into the sea off the *Pomboo*'s bow. It pops to the surface with a fat fish wiggling hard against its fate. The sea bird gags like a guy in a hotdog-eating contest. *Gulp.* Down goes the fish.

No trainer commanded this leap by a Shark Bay dolphin.

"Two new dolphins," Jenny calls out.

"It's Nicky and Fin," Janet says. "I don't believe this. They are way, way out of their normal range."

Little Fin joins Google. Nicky swims straight for the *Pomboo*.

"What are you doing, Nicky?" Janet asks.

But Janet knows exactly what Nicky is doing. Even I can read Nicky's body language. The speckle-bellied old lady swims close, turns slightly on her side, and half opens her mouth.

Got fish?

Janet mutters darkly about boaters who must be slipping treats to Nicky. Aside from the strictly regulated beach sessions, feeding Shark Bay dolphins is illegal. Yet some thoughtless people still do it.

Janet crosses her arms and frowns. "Go away, Nicky."

Nicky tries another pass, as if to say, *Are you SURE you haven't got fish?*

At last Nicky realizes that nobody's falling for her cute dolphin act. She doesn't bother visiting Bytefluke; she just swims off. Fin trails behind.

The clouds turn buttery in the late-afternoon sun. Bytefluke carries on sponging through water that shimmers like an opal. Rise . . . take a long, leaden breath . . . down again.

I ask Janet if Google has any brothers or sisters. She shakes her head sadly. "Bytefluke seems like such a good mom. But none of her other calves have made it."

The Shark Bay environment tests each dolphin; the most successful leave the most offspring. Yet so many things can happen over the course of a dolphin's long life — including plain bad luck.

Will Google, frisky son of hard-working Bytefluke, survive? What about Fin, neglected daughter of Nicky? Will she beat the odds?

Janet has followed these calves and scores of others since their birth. She doesn't know where the youngsters will end up. Can Cheeky fight off his mysterious skin disease? What will happen to the sons of spongers such as Guppy, Rang, and Google, who don't seem to sponge? How will their alliances play out? What about Kooks, who does sponge? Will Kooks be odd man out?

Wait a minute — is Kooks even *male*?

Humans, like dolphins, evolved in a challenging environment. The need to eat drove the smartest of us to develop foraging tools. We invented digging sticks to help uncover edible roots and used flaked stones to kill prey

Nicky comes around for another pass as Janet watches her from the *Pomboo. Pomboo* is "dolphin" in Swahili.

and cut hides. We passed our knowledge to our children. Living in small groups, we cooperated with others. *Help me today, and I'll help you tomorrow.* Yet we also competed—for the tastiest food, the best mates, the highest status. One hundred thousand years ago, as much as today, we needed to make complex choices. Intelligence gave us the ability to make better decisions. We remembered; we considered alternatives; we imagined different outcomes. We chose.

India must decide when to leave Puck's happy family and whom to ally with. Perhaps he'll hang out with Samu and Cheeky until they're old enough for prime-time pirating. Dodger will probably become fertile in the next year or so. Nobody yet knows what subtle power females have, but perhaps Dodger will choose the father of her calf from among the males who will herd her. Cookie, Smokey, and Real Notch will spend the rest of their conniving lives in a swirling blender of choices about friends and rivals.

Google doesn't seem too worried about his future. The youngster flips belly-up and glides toward the *Pomboo's* bow. He pauses to gaze at us through a flat pane of crystal water.

Nicky on the lookout for handouts.

How remarkable this is. Two species inhabiting mutually alien landscapes, yet both evolving intelligence as their solution to life's challenges. And coming together where air meets sea.

I wonder . . . Does Google look up and see fellow big-brained animals? Does he think, *Wow, there's something special about people?*

Nah. He probably just thinks we're goofy-looking.

We leave Google and Bytefluke and head for home. If the dolphins of Shark Bay have taught us anything, it's that they don't conform to our myths. Dolphins aren't noble elves in wetsuits. Like us, they are something far more interesting: creatures with lives juicy with drama and crammed with complications. And their big brains offer them the same thing our big brains offer us:

possibilities.

Google glides in front of the _Pomboo's_ bow.

MORE ABOUT DOLPHINS

Dolphin Echolocation

Many pregnant women receive sonograms. A sonogram converts sound waves into a picture, allowing doctors to check the health of an unborn baby. A sonogram, however, is much less sophisticated than dolphin echolocation.

Years ago, when people and dolphins mixed freely at Monkey Mia, Janet noticed a woman standing in waist-deep water. Nicky's mother, Holeyfin, swam in tight circles around the woman. Janet knew Holeyfin wasn't very friendly and showed interest in people only in one very specific condition.

Janet waded over. "Excuse me. When is your baby due?"

The woman glanced down at her flat stomach. "How could you know?" she gasped. "I haven't even told my husband yet!"

The mother-to-be splashed back to shore. Janet followed, guiltily trying to explain diagnosis by dolphin.

Threats to Dolphins

Shark Bay is remote and relatively untouched by human activities. The bottlenose dolphins living there are well protected. Many other dolphin populations are not as lucky.

More than 200,000 dolphins may die every year due to net entanglement. Although "dolphin safe" tuna fisheries exist and these fishers allow trapped dolphins to escape, entrapment in fishing nets is very stressful. The effect of this stress on dolphin mortality, particularly calf mortality, is unknown.

Water pollution is a growing threat to dolphins as the human population of coastal areas grows. Tiny fish contaminated by toxins are eaten by larger contaminated fish, which are eaten by dolphins, and the contaminants build up in the dolphin's body. When a female dolphin gives birth to her first calf, many of the toxins in her body are purged through nursing. In places like Sarasota, Florida, most firstborn calves die—poisoned by their own mother's milk.

Fishers in a few countries, notably Japan, slaughter dolphins for meat. Ironically, the meat isn't healthy to eat because of the toxins in the dolphins' tissues. A few of the dolphins captured in these hunts are sold to oceanariums and "swim with the dolphins" programs.

Communicating Ideas and Discoveries

When a scientist's research shows interesting results, the scientist writes an article (often referred to simply as a "paper") and submits it to a scientific journal. The editors of the journal send the paper to other scientists, who review the paper. If the scientist who wrote the paper hasn't provided enough evidence to support her conclusions, the paper will be rejected. The reviewers may tell the author that she needs to collect more data or do more data analysis before the paper can be published.

Sometimes scientific discoveries are also summarized and reported in the popular media (the Internet, television, newspapers, and magazines). Popular articles about Shark Bay dolphins can be found at **www.monkeymiadolphins.org/content/articles.**

The original source is best, though. You can read published scientific articles by Shark Bay Dolphin Project scientists at **www.monkeymiadolphins.org/content/publications.**

Among the 2005 publications you'll find Janet's study of calf deaths ("Surviving at Sea: Ecological and Behavioral Predictors of Calf Mortality in Indian Ocean Bottlenose Dolphins, *Tursiops sp.*"), described in Chapter 2. Look for Eric Patterson's paper on sponging described in Chapter 4 among the 2011 publications ("The Ecological Conditions That Favor Tool Use and Innovation in Wild Bottlenose Dolphins"). Janet's study of dolphin sponging culture, described in Chapter 7, is found in the 2012 publications ("Social Networks Reveal Cultural Behavior in Tool-Using Dolphins").

Sure, these papers are written for scientists. Most people won't read a real scientific paper until they're in college, and maybe not even then. Who cares? You may be surprised at how much you understand. The "Methods" and "Results" sections are the most technical, so it's okay to skip those and just read the introduction at the beginning of the paper and the discussion at the end.

Go ahead—give it a try.

Internet Resources

Visit the Shark Bay Dolphin Project at **www.monkeymiadolphins.org** for the latest Shark Bay news and research findings. The written source material for this book is online at **www.monkeymiadolphins.org/content/publications.**

The Shark Bay Ecosystem Research Project at **www2.fiu.edu/~heithaus/SBERP** has a great website with information on tiger sharks, dugongs, sea turtles, and more. Under "Teacher Resources" you'll find a complete lesson plan that uses the Shark Bay ecosystem to teach science standards.

If you are planning a visit to the Shark Bay area, the Monkey Mia Dolphin Resort information can be found at **www.monkeymia.com.au.**

For more information about this book, including a special peek at how survey and focal follow data are collected on Shark Bay dolphins, please visit my website at **www.pamelasturner.com.**

Books

Reiss, Diana. *The Dolphin in the Mirror: Exploring Dolphin Minds and Saving Dolphin Lives.* New York: Houghton Mifflin Harcourt, 2011.

Smolker, Rachel. *To Touch a Wild Dolphin: A Journey of Discovery with the Sea's Most Intelligent Creatures.* New York: Random House, 2001.

Multimedia

The Dolphins of Shark Bay. Big Wave
Productions Ltd., 2010. Produced
for the BBC and Animal Planet,
this documentary stars Janet,
Puck, and Samu. It also displays
Reggae's beach-hunting prowess.

Planet Earth. BBC, Warner, 2007. Yes,
that's star beach-hunter Reggae in
the "Shallow Seas" episode.

Private Lives of Dolphins. WGBH
Educational Foundation, 1992.
A NOVA documentary on the
complex social world of male
dolphins.

Encephalization Quotient (EQ) Sources

My information on EQ is drawn
from two papers by Lori Marino:
"Origin and Evolution of Large Brains
in Toothed Whales" (*Anatomical
Record*, Dec. 2004, pp. 1247–55) and
"Convergence of Complex Cognitive
Abilities in Cetaceans and Primates"
(*Brain, Behavior and Evolution*, 2002,
vol. 59, pp. 21–32).

From left
to right:
Photographer
Scott Tuason,
Jenny Smith,
Janet Mann,
Katie Gill,
Eric Patterson,
author Pamela
Turner, and
Kipp Searles.

Acknowledgments

First and foremost, this book could not have been written without Janet
Mann's generous help and guidance, including hundreds of pesky questions,
my visit to Monkey Mia, and reviews of drafts of this manuscript. My
heartfelt thanks to Janet's crew: Eric Patterson, Katie Gill, Jennifer Smith,
and Kipp Searles, all of whom make me believe in the future of science
and conservation. Richard Connor kindly explained some of the intricacies
of male alliances. The Shark Bay Dolphin Project database is the product
of thousands of hours of hard work by many researchers; my thanks to all
contributors, past and present.

Scott Tuason clicked away nonstop to shoot most of the photos for this
book. As always, I am grateful for his artistry and good company. My thanks to
Nick Stringer of Big Wave Productions, Ltd., the Shark Bay Dolphin Project,
Michael Heithaus, Simon Allen, Alison True, and Richard Woldendorp for
additional images.

The "Sharkies" of the Shark Bay Ecosystem Research Project were a
fountain of wisdom on all Shark Bay creatures, great and small. I am grateful
to the Department of Environment and Conservation of Western Australia,
the Monkey Mia Dolphin Resort, and Georgetown University for their
assistance.

This is my fourth Scientists in the Field with my talented editor and
fellow animal lover, Erica Zappy Wainer. I hope we can partner for many
more. The art director Scott Magoon and the designers at YAY! put together
a wonderful design for which I am extremely grateful. Many thanks also to
Caryn Wiseman of Andrea Brown Literary Agency. My critiquers (Carol
Peterson, Nancy Humphrey Case, Deborah Underwood, Keely Parrack, Luka
Morgan, Connie Goldsmith, Lynn Hazen, Anne Reilly, Ellen Yeoman, and
Lesley Mandros Bell) deserve a lot of credit for spurring me on while reining
in my worst literary habits. And to Ted Glattke: thanks for the pirate idea!

My deepest gratitude goes to my family: my husband, Rob, and my
children, Travis, Kelsey, and Connor, for their support and tolerance of my
various science-geek obsessions. Love to all of you.

Latest News

On the human side: Double congratula-
tions to Eric Patterson! He received his
Ph.D. in December 2012, and he and Katie
Gill were married in April 2013.

On the dolphin side: The young
dolphins featured in this book continue to
mature. India (Puck's son) has started hanging out with other males his age—"all boys
that try to act tough," according to Janet.
Cheeky's skin discoloration has faded, he
is now weaned, and Janet confirmed that
he is indeed a boy. Likewise, Kooks is
definitely a male. Google, son of Bytefluke,
has recently been observed with a sponge.
Fin, Nicky's daughter, is now weaned and
spends most of her time with Flute (Piccolo's daughter).

The mystery dolphin pictured on page
2 was later named Epicure, which means
someone who likes the good things in life.
Especially food.

The old pro Real Notch has gotten
even closer to his son Cookie. This has
resulted in Urchin spending more time
with Smokey and Lando. Those three need
to watch their backs.

Every year brings new babies. Piccolo
(daughter of Puck and Real Notch) gave
birth to Piper. Kiya (also a daughter of
Puck and Real Notch) gave birth to Wir-
riya. Nicky and another beach-fed mother,
Shock, have new calves too. Whoops,
daughter of Wedges, is now mother to a calf
named Whippet.

But I've saved the really big news for
last. Blip, who is at least forty-two years old,
is also a new mom! Janet calculates that
Blip got pregnant around the time when we
saw her being herded by the Prima Donnas.
Blip's surprise out-of-season calf was chris-
tened Blooper.

INDEX

Page numbers in **bold** refer to photos and illustrations.